EGGS

EGGS

the definitive cook's guide to choosing,
cooking and enjoying eggs

Alex Barker

LORENZ BOOKS

This edition is published by Lorenz Books

Lorenz Books is an imprint of Anness Publishing Ltd
Hermes House, 88–89 Blackfriars Road, London SE1 8HA
tel. 020 7401 2077; fax 020 7633 9499
www.lorenzbooks.com; info@anness.com

© Anness Publishing Ltd 2001, 2002

Published in the USA by Lorenz Books, Anness Publishing Inc.
27 West 20th Street, New York, NY 10011; fax 212 807 6813

Published in Australia by Lorenz Books, Anness Publishing Pty Ltd
Level 1, Rugby House, 12 Mount Street, North Sydney, NSW 2060
tel. (02) 8920 8622; fax (02) 8920 8633

This edition distributed in the UK by Aurum Press Ltd
25 Bedford Avenue, London WC1B 3AT
tel. 020 7637 3225; fax 020 7580 2469

This edition distributed in the USA by National Book Network
4720 Boston Way, Lanham, MD 20706
tel. 301 459 3366; fax 301 459 1705; www.nbnbooks.com

This edition distributed in Canada by General Publishing
895 Don Mills Road, 400–402 Park Centre, Toronto, Ontario M3C 1W3
tel. 416 445 3333; fax 416 445 5991; www.genpub.com

This edition distributed in New Zealand by David Bateman Ltd
30 Tarndale Grove, Off Bush Road, Albany, Auckland
tel. (09) 415 7664; fax (09) 415 8892

A CIP catalogue record for this book is available from the British Library.

Publisher: Joanna Lorenz
Managing Editor: Linda Fraser
Editor: Susannah Blake
Editorial reader: Richard McGinlay
Designer: Nigel Partridge
Photography: Amanda Heywood (recipes) and Steve Moss (reference)
Food for Photography: Joy Skipper (recipes) and Alex Barker and Stephanie England (reference)

Previously published as *Get Cracking*

1 3 5 7 9 10 8 6 4 2

NOTES

Bracketed terms are intended for American readers.

For all recipes, quantities are given in both metric and imperial measures and, where appropriate, measures are
also given in standard cups and spoons. Follow one set, but not a mixture, because they are not interchangeable.

Standard spoon and cup measures are level. 1 tsp = 5ml, 1 tbsp = 15ml, 1 cup = 250ml/8fl oz

Australian standard tablespoons are 20ml. Australian readers should use 3 tsp in place of 1 tbsp
for measuring small quantities of gelatine, flour, salt, etc.

Medium (US large) eggs are used unless otherwise stated.

The very young, the elderly, pregnant women and those in ill-health or with a compromised immune system are
advised against consuming raw eggs or dishes and drinks containing raw eggs.

Contents

INTRODUCTION

Egyptian and Chinese records show that fowl were laying eggs for man as early as 1400BC and the use of eggs in the kitchen has been noted since Greek and Roman times.

Chickens reared today are thought to have descended from the Red Jungle Fowl *Gallus*, a native of the Himalayas some 4,000 years ago. The birds were probably brought to Europe from Asia and were then taken to America by Christopher Columbus in 1493. By the 14th century, several types of eggs were being eaten, including those from the duck, goose, plover, seagull and a short-legged hen called a "creepie", which laid very small eggs.

In the Middle Ages, eggs were often poached, posing an interesting problem for those eating with fingers and sharing plates. However, from early records, one

Below: Poultry have been domesticated and farmed for their eggs for centuries.

of the most popular ways of cooking eggs was in the ashes of a softwood fire. John Cardy Jeaffreson, a late 19th-century author on social history, included the following quotation in *A Book About the Table*, published in 1875: "The peasant who bakes his egg in hot wood embers piled about the shell, knows by a sure sign when the meat is sufficiently cooked. As soon as a clear dew-drop exudes from the shell's top, visible above the embers, the egg is done to the perfection of softness."

In total contrast, by the time Jeaffreson was writing on the history of egg cooking, eggs were in use in lavish dishes in the Victorian kitchen. Mrs Beeton, the famous author of the *Book of Cookery and Household Management*, wrote that every good cook needs "an ample sufficiency of eggs with cream and new milk". It was the Victorians who introduced the idea of eating eggs for breakfast. Whatever else was eaten,

Above: Throughout history, eggs have been considered as a source of food. This 13th-century manuscript depicts a group of women buying eggs.

in genteel households, each morning the cook would coddle a cluster of fresh eggs in an elaborate china hen to greet the family when they sat down to breakfast. Trays taken to those who opted for breakfast in the privacy of their bed chambers included eggs nestling under cosies – thick woollen coats designed to retain the heat, not the dainty egg cosies we know today.

Throughout history, eggs have been associated with the universe, creation and new life. The Egyptians believed that their God, Ptah, created the egg out of the sun and the moon and the Phoenicians thought that two halves of a very large egg had split open to produce heaven and earth. Similarly, in Chinese legend, the universe was egg-shaped, with the yolk representing the earth and the white the heavens. Early man separated the yolk from the white, introducing the idea of the white, the clear element, as yang and the yolk, the dark murky earth, as yin. To the Chinese, the egg is a symbol of fertility, so when a child is born the parents give dyed eggs as gifts to friends.

Because of its connection with new life, the egg has often been thought of as an aphrodisiac and a fertility aid. In

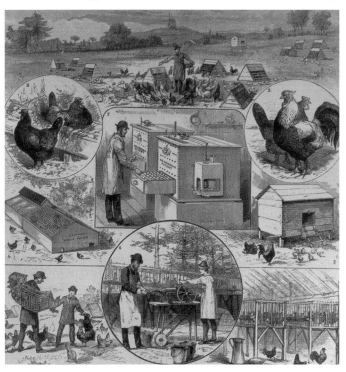

Above, clockwise from top left: Bantam eggs, hen's eggs, pullet's eggs, quail's eggs and white hen's eggs

Central Europe, farmers would rub eggs on their ploughs hoping to improve the crops and in France, brides would break an egg on the doorstep of their new home to ensure a large family.

Egg painting is an art around the world. In Japan eggs are painted red as tokens of luck and joy. Coloured eggs often feature in Jewish and Middle Eastern religious festivals. Jewish *haminodos* are baked with onions or saffron until they are rich golden, rust or red in colour. One traditional recipe for these shiny exotic eggs runs as follows. "Mix equal proportions olive oil and Turkish coffee. Put in this mixture as many eggs as requested, in their shells, and cook them on a very slow fire for twelve hours. The mixture will penetrate the shells, give the white an

amber colour, the yolks the colour of saffron, and the eggs will have the taste of the most delicious chestnuts you have ever eaten."

For centuries, eggs have had a religious or spiritual significance attached to them. To the early Egyptians, Persians, Romans and Greeks, the egg was symbolic of the universe and continuing life and represented the sun of spring. Eggs

have long been associated with new life at Easter after the fasting of Lent. In Mediterranean countries, sweet Easter breads, such as Greek *tsoureki*, are baked and adorned with brightly painted or dyed eggs, and chocolate eggs, although a modern addition to Easter celebrations, are also popular. Similar associations between life and fertility are made in Judaism, during the Passover celebrations.

Eggs are not only eaten at Easter but they also feature in traditional seasonal games. Easter egg hunts; egg tapping, sometimes a very messy game; and egg rolling, usually ending with a race down a hill or across a garden, are just a few examples. These and other games are part of the annual Easter festivities attended by the President at the White House in the United States of America.

Left: Egg painting has long been a tradition in many cultures.

THE STRUCTURE OF THE EGG

The shell Hens today produce eggs that are two or three times larger than those produced by their ancestors. Surprisingly, the actual amount of shell has not increased, resulting in eggs with a much thinner, more delicate shell. Luckily, with domesticated hens, the shell is no longer needed to protect the chick from would-be aggressors. The egg shell makes up 12 per cent of the total weight of the egg and is composed largely of calcium. Its strength is influenced by the hen's diet and age. Larger hens produce larger eggs with thinner shells. The shell is porous, allowing moisture out and air in, which is vital for the early development of the chick. The shell is also covered with a protective coating, which helps to prevent bacteria entering the egg.

The air cell The inside of the shell is lined with two very thin membranes. At the rounded end of the egg, the membranes separate slightly to produce a space that is filled with air. As the egg ages, moisture and carbon dioxide pass through the pores of the shell and are replaced by more air, which collects in the space. As the air cell grows, the egg becomes lighter and will eventually float if placed in a glass of water.

The white This is the albumen and it makes up about 67 per cent of the egg's total weight. It is transluscent when uncooked and contains over half of the protein found in an egg. It is thicker immediately around a fresh yolk while the outer part of the white is thinner. As the egg ages, the distinction between these two layers of white diminishes. Twisted strands run through the white to anchor the yolk in place. These are the chalazae and the more prominent they are, the fresher the egg. Although the chalazae do not affect the cooking qualities of the egg, you may prefer to strain them out of custards and sauces as they can set in fine strings that spoil the eating quality of smooth mixtures.

Below: The colour of an egg's shell is determined solely by the breed of bird.

The yolk Surrounded by a membrane, the yolk makes up about a third of the egg. It contains all the fat, just less than half the protein, all the vitamins A, D and E and most of the minerals that can be found in an egg. The colour of the yolk depends purely on the diet of a hen. A diet rich in yellow corn will produce medium-yellow yolks. Natural foods colours, such as nasturtiums, can be added to produce the popular rich yellow colour. Yolks occasionally have blood spots on them and, although unsightly, are just a sign of freshness and do not indicate that the egg has been fertilized. If you find these spots unappetizing, they can be removed very easily before cooking.

THE NUTRITIONAL VALUE OF EGGS

Often referred to as the most complete and pure food, eggs contain everything needed for the growth of the young chick and this also provides a very good source of food for humans. Eggs are primarily a protein food, and the protein they provide contains all eight amino acids that are essential for growth and repair of the body. Because it is of such high quality, egg protein is used as the standard by which to measure the value of other protein foods. One medium (US large) egg will provide 12–14 per cent of the recommended daily allowance of protein for an adult.

An egg contains fat in the yolk, but it is not a high-fat food. A medium egg yolk contains about 1.6g fat, just over 50 per cent of which is unsaturated, with 29 per cent saturated fatty acids.

Eggs contain varying amounts of 13 vitamins, most importantly vitamins D, A and E and many of the B vitamins. However, eggs do not contain any vitamin C.

Eggs are also a useful source of minerals, including phosphorus, iron and calcium, and the essential trace elements zinc, iodine and selenium. The amount of calcium is small, with a medium egg providing about 3 per cent of the daily recommended intake.

The energy provided by an egg varies from 66Kcals/276kJ for a small egg to 94Kcals/394kJ for a very large egg.

Above: There is no difference in the nutritional value of white or brown eggs.

HANDLING EGGS

Eggs should be stored at a constant temperature, preferably below 8°C/46.5°F. Hands, work surfaces and equipment should be cleaned thoroughly after cooking with eggs to prevent potential contamination of bacteria from eggs to other foods that may be eaten raw.

WHITE VERSUS BROWN

There is no difference in the nutritional value of white or brown eggs. The colour of the shell is determined by the breed of hen. Breeds with white feathers and ear lobes, such as Leghorn, lay white eggs. Breeds with red feathers and red ear lobes, such as Rhode Island Red or Plymouth Rock, lay brown eggs. White eggs are preferred in the United States, with a few exceptions, including New England, where brown eggs are more popular. The colour of the yolk is influenced by diet, and feed that is high in corn will result in very yellow egg yolks.

DOUBLE THE VALUE

Double-yolked eggs are the result of two egg cells maturing at the same time. The two cells pass through the hen's reproductive system together and are surrounded by a single white and shell. They are usually produced by young hens whose reproductive cycles are not fully synchronized.

Below: Occasionally, you may find an egg that contains two yolks within a single white.

CHOLESTEROL

This fat-like substance is produced naturally in the body and found in the blood. It is essential for body cells, digestive juices and hormones, but the body can have too much. Cholesterol is found in egg yolk, but not in the white. If you are on a low-fat diet, particularly to help control blood cholesterol levels, you should limit egg consumption to no more than one a day.

SALMONELLA

These bacteria are found in poultry and on the surface of other raw meats. They can cause severe food poisoning if they are present in high numbers when food is eaten. Although infected hens can contaminate eggs, recently instigated quality controls have reduced this risk. Careful handling, rigorous inspection and control of all sources of raw meat are measures now in place. Imported products are also subject to tight control, especially those from countries that have poor contamination records. Constant storage at or below 20°C/68°F is enforced to prevent bacteria from multiplying. The Lion code of practice used in the UK is being adopted by other countries, so all young hens that are bred for egg production are vaccinated against salmonella.

It is generally recommended that raw eggs should not be served to the very young, the elderly or to those in ill-health or with a compromised immune system. Thoroughly cooking eggs at a temperature above 60°C/140°F will ensure that bacteria are killed off. Eggs can sometimes be lightly cooked for use in recipes that traditionally use raw eggs. Meringues can be made using a hot syrup, whisked over hot water, and yolks can be heated very gently with a minimum of 30ml/2 tbsp liquid per yolk, stirring continuously, until the mixture coats the back of a spoon or reaches a temperature of 71°C/160°F.

CHOOSING, USING AND COOKING WITH EGGS

When people think of eggs they think of the hen's eggs included in their weekly shopping. However, there are many other, more unusual varieties that are becoming more readily available, such as pheasant and guinea fowl eggs, or even gull's eggs. This chapter gives fascinating information on the types of eggs available, their appearance and flavour, and advice on where to buy them and how to store them. There is also invaluable guidance on how to test the freshness of an egg, its cooking properties, and the range of cooking equipment available to achieve great results.

VARIETIES OF EGGS

Hen's eggs are part of the regular diet for most of the world's population and there are many countries that regard any eggs as a source of food. Third World countries and areas with large peasant populations, particularly where food is scarce, still regard any form of protein food as very important. Eggs from the blackbird, fulmar, gannet, guillemot, gull, penguin, plover, puffin, swan, thrush and more are all eaten. In some parts of the world, any nest that can be reached is a potential source of food. Many stories tell of the delicious nature of wild birds' eggs. In countries that do not suffer food shortages, collecting wild birds' eggs is now illegal as, with a few exceptions, wild or game birds' eggs are protected.

Below: Contented Rhode Island Reds peck their way around the farmyard.

Even the most unlikely eggs are a delicacy to some gourmets, as the following description reveals. "Penguins' eggs are laid in holes in the ground on the little Guano Islands off the coast of South Africa, they are delicious when perfectly fresh, plain hard boiled and cold; they much resemble plovers' eggs in taste and texture and are equal in bulk to about three of the latter."

Of course it is not only birds' eggs that are eaten. Turtle eggs are a delicacy around the many islands of the Pacific and the warmer parts of the Atlantic, where they are considered to be an aphrodisiac; they are also a prized ingredient in Asian cooking. Round, white and shaped like ping-pong balls, turtle eggs are soft-shelled and delicious baked in bamboo leaves over the fire. They are a treat local inhabitants might occasionally allow

themselves, though they would never take more than a few eggs from the nest at any time. Poachers, on the other hand, are not as scrupulous and have endangered the species by lying in wait for the female turtle to lay anything up to 200 eggs in a night in sandy hollows above the water line, before they take all the eggs. International laws are now in place to prevent this profiteering and to counteract the destruction of the life cycle of the turtle. Other reptile eggs are also enjoyed in Asia.

Fish eggs are highly prized. Sturgeon eggs, known as caviar, are the most famous and expensive. These shiny black, salty eggs are adored by the Russians and cost a small fortune per teaspoonful. Shiny red salmon eggs, also known as caviar, are less expensive and have become fashionable, mainly for their colour.

Above: When available, bantam eggs are a good choice for young children because of their small size.

HEN'S EGGS

These eggs are produced by the billion each year. Domesticated hens are the most prolific producers of eggs for culinary use around the world. Of the many hundreds of breeds of hen, only a handful are actually reared for commercial egg production. The breed has to be chosen for the specific environment in which it is to be reared and for the eggs it lays, as they must be suitable for selling. Cross-breeds from the popular Rhode Island Red, such as Isabrown, Hy-Line and Babcock, are the source of the majority of commercial eggs, but small farms and specialist breeders sometimes rear some of the more romantically named hens, such as Black Maran, Brahma, Indian Game, Buff Orpington, Plymouth Rock and Silkie. Silkies produce very small dainty

Right: A medium hen's egg weighs about 50g/2oz.

white eggs, which are good for baking and for children's meals. Rhode Island Reds are excellent layers and produce the classic light brown egg. Other breeds, such as Marans, lay speckled, deep tan to dark brown eggs, while Araucanas lay eggs that are a very pale blue.

Above: Eggs vary in size and colour, depending on the breed of bird.

BANTAM EGGS

Being about half the size of hens, bantams produce much smaller eggs. In some cases, bantams are natural dwarf animals or they may be specially bred miniatures of the larger breeds. Their eggs have a similar flavour to hen's eggs and can be used in the same way as full-size eggs, but you will need to double the number of eggs required in the recipe. Bantams are kept by small or specialist farmers, so their eggs are not widely available. They can sometimes be found in farm stores.

Left: A bantam egg is about half the size of a hen's egg.

Above: Quail's eggs are valued for their appearance as well as their flavour.

QUAIL'S EGGS

These tiny eggs are about one-third of the size of hen's eggs and are readily available in stores and supermarkets. They are the smallest of all commercial eggs. They have dark-speckled, pale shells and make an attractive garnish when served in the half shell. The shelled eggs are also excellent in appetizers and canapés, or as a garnish. If they are not overcooked by boiling until too hard, they have a light, almost creamy texture and flavour. Quail's eggs can be poached and cooked in the same way as hen's eggs.

DUCK EGGS

Domesticated ducks originated from wild waterfowl. Their eggs are bigger than hen's eggs, weighing about 90g/3½oz, and their shell colour can vary from shades of very pale green-blue to white. They have a slightly higher fat content and oilier texture than hen's eggs. They are richer in flavour,

Left: A tiny quail's egg weighs about 20g/¾oz.

which makes them ideal for baking, but the whites are firmer and slightly rubbery in texture when set, so they are not to everyone's taste when plainly cooked. Their rich yellow yolks produce wonderfully golden sponges but the whites are unsuitable for meringues.

Duck eggs are often laid in muddy places, so they should be always be washed and thoroughly cooked. A

Right: A duck egg is about the same size as a very large hen's egg.

boiling time of at least 10 minutes is recommended. These eggs are available mainly from speciality food stores, butchers, fishmongers and delicatessens. They should be stored in the refrigerator and eaten as soon as possible. For a better result, allow duck eggs to return to room temperature before cooking.

Left: Duck eggs come in translucent shades of blue, green and white.

Below: Domesticated ducks can be very good layers.

GOOSE EGGS

Geese are notorious for being unfriendly and extremely noisy and are sometimes said to be a good alternative to guard dogs. Their eggs are at least twice the size of hen's eggs, weighing about 200g/7oz each, and are a pure, chalky white. The shells of goose eggs are usually very hard. Geese are fairly messy birds so, like duck eggs, goose eggs need washing and thorough cooking to kill any harmful bacteria that may be lurking on their shells.

Although they are stronger in flavour than hen's eggs, goose eggs are slightly milder than duck eggs and are not as rich. They can be cooked simply and eaten on their own, but they are particularly good as an ingredient in mildly flavoured baked dishes, such as vegetable gratins and quiches.

Goose eggs are available in season from specialist butchers, delicatessens and farm stores.

Left: Geese are well-known for their aggressive nature so it is a good idea to keep a safe distance.

Below: The shells of goose eggs are pure white and very hard.

Below: A goose egg is twice the size of a hen's egg and weighs about 200g/7oz.

Above and below: Turkey eggs are slightly larger than hen's eggs and have an attractive speckled shell.

Above: Guinea fowl eggs are a similar size to bantam eggs and weigh about 25g/1oz each.

GUINEA FOWL EGGS

These birds are related to pheasants and chickens. Their eggs are roughly half the size of hen's eggs and weigh about 25g/1oz each. They are light brown and very regular in colour. Guinea fowl eggs have a light and delicate flavour. They are ideal for garnishing dishes or adding to salads and are also good for baking. They are available from specialist breeders.

TURKEY EGGS

These eggs weigh about 75g/3oz and have creamy white shells with light brown speckles. The smaller eggs of young birds tend to be paler than those of older birds. Although turkeys are farmed in most parts of the world, their eggs are rarely available. The birds are usually bred for their meat so their eggs are kept for hatching. However, outside the main breeding season you may find a local farmer who has some to spare. There is little difference in taste between turkey and hen's eggs and they are good for baking.

Left: Pheasant egg

PHEASANT EGGS

These eggs are of a similar size to those of guinea fowl. They vary in colour from buff to green-blue or olive and can be speckled. They have quite a strong flavour and can be boiled for use in salads, baked or cooked in most other ways. They are available from game dealers and some farm stores. Crack each egg into a cup before adding to other ingredients in case it is bad.

OSTRICH EGGS

Since ostrich meat has grown in popularity, ostrich eggs have become increasingly available. An ostrich egg weighs 450g/1lb or more. It has a comparatively strong flavour and is best used in baking. The pale shells are very thick and hard to crack. Laying is seasonal, during summer and the eggs are usually sold by breeders, delicatessens and specialist stores.

Above: Pheasant eggs are smaller than hen's eggs and have a much more pronounced flavour.

EMU EGGS

The Australian emu is slightly smaller than the ostrich. They are protected in their natural habitat and a special licence is needed for collecting their eggs. However, emus are occasionally farmed for their meat and eggs. They have a winter laying season, during which time one bird will lay about 20 dark blue-green eggs, which have very hard shells. They are best used in baking but they can be scrambled or cooked in savoury dishes.

WILD BIRD EGGS

In most Western countries the eggs of wild birds are protected by legislation preventing their collection as a blanket measure to protect birds whose population is in decline. However, special licences are available for collecting the eggs from gulls, such as the great black-backed gull, the lesser black-backed gull and the herring gull. Gull's eggs are now eaten instead of plover eggs, which used to be considered a great delicacy. Gull's eggs are dark spotted green and brown and they have a mild fishy flavour. On some islands in the North of Scotland, it is possible to obtain a licence to collect gannet and fulmar eggs. Wild bird's eggs are available in season from specialist food stores and game dealers.

Left: An ostrich egg weighs about the same as 9–10 hen's eggs.

Left: An emu egg has an incredibly hard shell.

BUYING AND STORING EGGS

Many bird's eggs are edible but, in the the kitchen, an egg usually means a hen's egg. There is a wide range of eggs available, such as organic eggs; vegetarian eggs (from hens on a diet free of fishmeal or bonemeal); eggs from hens reared on other types of diet; double-yolked eggs; eggs nutritionally enhanced with omega-3 fatty acids; and even eggs marked as "breakfast eggs" or "weekend eggs". There is also a choice of free-range, barn or cage-produced eggs.

After World War II, the need to increase food production brought about the change to housing chickens in battery cages. These increased production and helped to control disease, but by the 1980s the public became aware of the terrible conditions in which chickens were kept. They were housed high off the ground, in pens from which they could not escape, and

with about 14,000 birds to a single hen-house. The realization of the conditions endured by the miserable birds, combined with scares for food safety from increased cases of salmonella, made consumers acutely aware of the cruelty and food safety issues involved.

The image of these birds has put many people off economy eggs and created greater demand for free-range eggs. Some improvements have now been made to the battery system and they are closely monitored and updated throughout the European Union (EU). At the same time, doubts have been raised about the hygiene standards of free-range egg production methods.

EGG PRODUCTION METHODS

Hens (pullets) start laying at about 20 weeks old and increase their laying until they lay every day at about 25 weeks old. This continues for 13–15 weeks,

then the laying declines. The average bird now lays about 290 eggs in the first 52 weeks, compared with 123 eggs, which was the average between 1945–6. Eggs are either collected manually and then sorted by eye or, more often, they are collected automatically by conveyor belt leading directly from the laying houses to the packing area.

There is a worldwide dilemma over egg production. The five main egg production methods are free-range, semi-intensive, deep litter, perchery (barn) and caged. In both the EU and the USA, legislation has been developed to clarify all methods of egg production. The Farm Animal Welfare Council, the Royal Society for the Prevention of Cruelty to Animals and several other

Below: Free-range hens are able to wander freely around the farmyard.

animal welfare groups have developed the Freedom Food approval scheme and such groups continue to strive for the improvement of conditions for egg production all over the world. However, about 80 per cent of all eggs are still produced by the cage system.

Free-range This method allows hens to have continuous access to open-air runs that are mainly covered with vegetation. There may be a maximum of 395 hens per acre of ground, which allows slightly more than 10sq m/ 108sq ft per bird. The buildings must meet certain conditions, such as a constant temperature and a continuous water supply.

Semi-intensive Similar to free-range, this method reduces the space per bird to a minimum of 2.5sq m/9½sq ft.

Deep litter This housed system allows a maximum of 7 hens per sq m/sq yd and at least one-third of the floor must be covered with straw or shavings.

Perchery or barn This is a system based on specially designed units with a maximum of 25 birds per sq metre/ sq yd floor space and at least 15cm/ 6in perch space per hen.

Cage This system allows 3–5 hens per cage, with 450sq cm/70sq in per bird with plans to increase the space to 550sq cm/85sq in per bird.

Enriched cages This new scheme will allow 750sq cm/116sq in per bird.

EGG GRADING

Eggs are graded at the packing station, where they are checked for both exterior and interior quality.

In a process known as candling, a light is shone through the eggs so that the contents can be checked without cracking the shell. Modern machinery enables the candler to view the contents of the egg, including the size of the air sac, and automatically remove any eggs with blood spots or imperfections.

If you keep chickens, you can check the internal quality of an egg by holding it up to a candle flame or a bright light in a darkened room. The shell should become sufficiently transparent for you to see if the egg is clear, whether it is fertilized or if there is a blood spot.

Above: During egg candling, an electric light is shone through whole eggs to allow the candler to view their contents.

These blood spots are caused by ruptured blood vessels on the yolk's surface and are not harmful. They are only visible in very fresh eggs and, contrary to popular belief, do not indicate that the egg is fertilized.

Only grade A (EU) or grade A and AA (USA) eggs reach the shops. In the USA, the eggs are washed and, as this removes their natural protective bloom, a light tasteless mineral oil is usually applied before packing. This application of oil is not permitted in the EU. The remaining eggs go to the catering trade; to manufacturing industries for pasteurized egg products; or are used for industrial purposes, rather than human consumption.

A grade These eggs may be called "Fresh" or, if collected daily, "Extra Fresh". Individual countries have their own national marking and quality guide systems in addition to this EU system. For instance, the Lion Quality is used in the UK and is stamped on the box of 70 per cent of all UK boxed eggs. It indicates that the eggs are fully traceable back to their parent flock, including the feed used. It guarantees that all the pullets in the flock have been vaccinated against salmonella and that the eggs have been transported and stored at temperatures of 20ºC/ 68ºF or below. These eggs also carry a "best before" date stamp on their shells, which should not exceed 21 days after the egg has been laid.

Loose eggs For those eggs sold unpacked, all information on the producer, quality, weight, best before date and storage advice must be displayed at the point of sale.

Below: Blood spots are caused by ruptured blood vessels. Contrary to popular belief, they are not a sign that an egg has been fertilized.

Left: (left to right) The most commonly available sizes of hen's egg are large, medium and small.

When buying eggs from a farm store, you may need to look more closely for dirt and cracks. Although controls over eggs sold in farm stores are not as rigid, they should still be refrigerated, or kept at a maximum of 20°C/68°F, even if they are very fresh.

Eggs from birds other than chickens, such as bantams, ducks or guinea fowl, are not subject to the same regulations and quality control, so be careful when buying them. The farm should be able to tell when they were collected and, if they have a good turnover, there should be no need for concern.

In the case of wild fowl, such as pheasants, the game keeper may not know when the eggs were laid, so take extra care to ensure that they are still fresh, especially in warmer weather. Crack each egg into a bowl before adding to other ingredients so that any bad ones can be discarded.

Below: Always check boxes of eggs for cracked ones before you buy.

EGG SIZING

The size of an egg can be influenced by a number of factors. The age of a hen is very important, with older hens tending to produce larger eggs. Other contributory factors include breed, weight, diet and stress. Eggs are sized by minimum weight. Small, medium and large are the most common sizes. Size does not make any difference when you are cooking a specific number of eggs, for example when frying, poaching or boiling them. However, when baking, the size of egg can be important because many recipes require accurate proportions of ingredients. Use the chart below to check that you are using the right weight of egg even if you cannot buy the right size.

DATE MARKING

Producers outside USA or EU inspection areas are governed by the laws in their own country or state. In the USA and EU, all boxes of eggs must be date marked. The date of packing, known as the Julian date, is used in the USA. This system gives each day of the year a separate number: day 1 refers to

eggs packed on 1st January and day 365 to those packed on 31st December. Boxes may also carry an expiry date after which the eggs cannot be sold. This "best before" date allows for seven days in a home environment after purchase when the eggs are safe to eat. In addition, the laying date and "sell by" or packing date can be stamped on to the shells in the EU and USA.

CHOOSING EGGS

With all the quality controls that are in operation, there should be little need for thorough checking, but it is always worth looking in the box to make sure that all the eggs are intact and that none are cracked or damaged. You should also check the date stamped on the box or egg, looking for the best before date, sell by date or date of packing. This will help you to work out how fresh the eggs are. Try to buy eggs from a shop that has a fast turnover so that they are really fresh when you buy them. Avoid buying eggs that are already two weeks old unless you know that you will be able to use them within a day or two.

Minimum Weight	EU Classification	USA Classification
73g/2½oz	XL (very large)	Jumbo
63g/2¼oz	L (large)	X Large
53g/2oz	M (medium)	Large
45g/1¾oz	S (Small)	Medium
40g/1½oz		Small
35g/1¼oz		Peewee

STORING FRESH EGGS

Egg shells are porous, making eggs vulnerable to bacteria and odours, which can be absorbed by the egg. To protect them from any smells that can affect their flavour, they should be stored in their box or in a special egg compartment in the refrigerator, at or below 4°C/40°F. Stored at the right temperature, an egg that is a week old can appear fresher than a day-old egg kept at room temperature. In these conditions eggs can be stored safely for 3–4 weeks. Remove eggs from the refrigerator shortly before using them, especially when making meringues, as a better result is often achieved if the eggs are at room temperature.

If you regularly use eggs very quickly and have a suitable cool area, away from sunlight, but well ventilated with fresh air, then the eggs can be stored in wire or wicker baskets or in their box. They will keep for about a week, as long as the temperature is at or below 20°C/68°F and does not fluctuate.

Although eggs should normally be kept away from strong aromas because of their ability to absorb smells, they can be flavoured intentionally. One of

the most well-known methods of flavouring fresh eggs is placing a whole fresh truffle in the egg box for 3–4 days. The delicious, earthy aroma of the truffle will permeate the shell and delicately flavour the egg.

Above: Eggs should be stored unwashed and with the pointed end down to reduce evaporation.

STORING COOKED EGGS

Whole eggs should only be stored if fully cooked through. If hard-boiled (hard-cooked) eggs are left in their shells, they will develop a dark ring around the yolk, which can look unappetizing.

Shelled eggs can be stored in the refrigerator, loosely wrapped in clear film for 1–2 days, but they will acquire a sulphurous smell. If they are to be used in sandwich fillings, for instance, make up the mixture with the freshly cooked egg, then cool and store in the refrigerator in a well-sealed container.

Omelettes and pancakes, which are intended for use in salads or toppings, can be kept in the refrigerator for 1–2 days. Chill well, then cover closely in clear film. Do not season the eggs before cooking as they are likely to need more seasoning before serving. Strong flavours, such as onion and garlic can affect other foods in the refrigerator.

Left: Eggs can be stored for a few days in a wicker basket in a cool, well-ventilated room.

STORING LEFTOVERS

When you need only the yolk or the white, the remaining part of the egg can be stored in the refrigerator for several days until required in another recipe. The yolk can be used to enrich sauces or pastry or make some mayonnaise. Leftover egg white can be used to make a small amount of meringue to top a baked apple or small fruit tarts. Label stored eggs with the quantity and date from the egg box. If you forget to put the number of whites or yolks on the label, remember that an egg weighs about 50g/2oz and the yolk weighs slightly less than half of that. Weigh the yolks or whites to work out how many you have.

To store egg whites, place them in a plastic container or thoroughly cleaned glass jar and cover.

Above: Whole eggs can be stored in an airtight container in the refrigerator.

Below: Egg whites can be frozen in a small airtight container.

Above: Covering the egg yolk with cold water will prevent it from hardening.

A tough, thick skin forms on whole yolks when they are exposed to air – even the air inside a container is enough to do this. Put the yolks in the smallest container you can find, then pour in enough cold water to cover the yolks and cover the container. To use the yolks, carefully drain off the water.

Beat broken yolks with 15–30ml/ 1–2 tbsp cold water, put into a small container and cover tightly.

FREEZING EGGS

Uncooked eggs that have been removed from their shells can be packed into small sealed containers and frozen. Try to use a container that is just large enough for the egg, so that it contains the minimum of air. Always label containers with the number of eggs and the date. To defrost, place in the refrigerator and leave overnight. Use as soon as possible.

Above: Protect beaten eggs from drying out by covering with clear film.

How to freeze eggs

1 Lightly beat whole eggs until yolks and whites are blended and pack in small containers.

2 Yolks and whites can be frozen separately in small containers. Yolks thicken on freezing, so beat lightly, adding 0.75ml/⅛ tsp salt or 7.5ml/1½ tsp sugar to every 4 yolks. Pack in small containers and label with the date, whether salt or sugar was added and the number of yolks.

3 If you often use eggs in small quantities, or for faster freezing and thawing, pack them in ice-cube trays and cover tightly with clear film. When frozen, transfer the cubes to plastic freezer bags.

4 Cooked whole eggs do not freeze successfully. Hard-boiled (hard-cooked) egg whites will become tough, rubbery and watery but hard-boiled yolks can freeze well if all the air is excluded.

Above: Lightly beaten whole eggs can be frozen in ice-cube trays.

TESTING FOR FRESHNESS

As soon as the egg is laid, moisture begins to evaporate through the porous shell. Air enters the egg and starts the natural process of deterioration. The warmer the egg, the faster the rate of deterioration. As the egg ages, the membranes that separate the various elements of the egg begin to soften, causing the egg to become flabby.

Above: A fresh egg will sink to the bottom in a glass of water.

Above: The older the egg, the lighter and more buoyant it is.

Above: A very fresh egg has a plump yolk and two distinct layers of white.

Above: A 12-day old egg will have a flatter yolk.

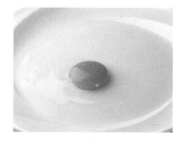

Above: A 21-day old egg will lose the definition between the layers of white.

Extremely fresh eggs taste delicious and are perfect for poaching, frying and scrambling because they hold together so well. However, if you need to separate whites from yolks, eggs of at least two days old are best. At this stage the whites will not have started to deteriorate but the whites and yolks will not be held together so firmly. As the eggs get older still and the membrane around the yolk deteriorates, you run the risk of breaking the yolk.

Although freshness does not influence the nutritional value of eggs, it does affect their cooking quality. Older eggs spread, looking flatter and flabbier when poached or fried, but they are easier to peel when hard-boiled (hard-cooked). For hard-boiled eggs, use eggs that are one to two weeks old because their air sac will have grown larger pushing the egg further from the shell and making it easier to peel.

To check the age of an unlabelled egg, crack the egg on a saucer: a fresh one will have a plump rounded yolk, sitting up well within two distinct layers of white; a 10–12 day old egg will have a far flatter yolk and less definition between the two layers of white; and a 21–28 day old egg will have lost the definition between the separate layers of white, which will have relaxed and blended into each other.

It is also possible to check how fresh an egg is without breaking it first. Place the egg in its shell in a glass of cold water. A very fresh egg will contain only a small air sac, so it will be heavier and should lie flat at the bottom of the glass. A very old egg will have a larger air sac, it will weigh less and it will be more buoyant at the blunt end of the egg that contains the air sac. An older egg will settle part way up the water or, if it is extremely old, it will float. If the egg floats it has probably gone bad and should be discarded.

How old is too old?
The recommendation for stores is only to sell eggs that are less than 21 days old. This recommendation is very safe. If eggs are stored under correct conditions, they can be safe for up to 28 days. If you have an egg that may be older than this, you should do one of the above tests before using. However, it is advisable to err on the side of caution and just throw it away. If you are in any doubt, break each egg individually into a cup before mixing it with any other ingredients. The smell will be your final test.

PRESERVED EGGS

Prior to intensive production, hens laid only during warmer weather and eggs had to be stored for the winter. Before freezing and drying were perfected, the most popular method of preserving eggs was in waterglass, a bacteria-resistant solution of sodium silicate, which prevented both the passage of bacteria and the evaporation of the egg content through the porous shell. The eggs were kept in the liquid in a cool place and could be stored for 8–9 months.

Various substances were painted over egg shells in attempts to seal them and prevent deterioration, but the only successful products were oil and petroleum jelly; both of which are still in controlled use today.

The oldest methods of storing eggs must be those used by Chinese cooks, who have preserved and bottled eggs for centuries. Salted eggs are hard-boiled (hard-cooked) in their shells and coated in a paste of earth and salt, wrapped in rice husks or grass and tightly packed in a large urn or pan. This is covered tightly and then left in a cold dark place for 30–40 days. These eggs are often used in festive cakes and when they are cut, their bright yellow yolks are revealed. Thousand-year-old

eggs are prepared in a similar way. They are smothered in a paste of wood ash and lime which turns them a dramatic brown-green colour. The shells need to be soaked before peeling, to allow them to soften. These eggs are eaten with soy sauce and sesame oil. They can also be stir-fried with pork and soy sauce or served as a garnish. If stored untouched, they can last for 2–3 months after preparation.

Above: Thousand-year-old eggs (left) and salted duck eggs take about 40 days to prepare.

Left: Thousand-year-old eggs are turned a translucent brown-green colour by the lime and wood ash paste in which they are coated.

EGG PRODUCTS

Various processed forms of egg are available for catering and, to a lesser extent, for use at home. In some countries, such as the UK, where salmonella scares have created demand, pasteurized egg products, using both whole and separated eggs, are available for baking, batters and meringues.

Dried or dehydrated egg was first available during World War II as part of rationing, then it fell out of use until recent years. Dried eggs are now widely used as an ingredient in packet convenience mixes. Dried egg white and whole egg are also available, although less common than specific recipe mixes. Dried whole egg is pasteurized and does not contain added ingredients, so it is ideal for people in weak health who are advised to avoid lightly cooked fresh eggs.

Speciality egg products, which are mainly available to the catering and food service industries, include omelettes, scrambled eggs, French toast, quiches and pancakes.

Modern dried egg products are very easy to use and, compared with the dried egg used in World War II, taste very similar to fresh eggs. Dried egg white, in particular, makes an excellent alternative to fresh, with no difference in taste at all. Dried meringue and royal icing (frosting) mixes produce admirable results and have the advantage of easy long-term storage. They are ready on the shelf when you need them and are ideal if you only want to use small quantities at a time. Dried whole egg is ideal for scrambling, omelettes and baking. It is simply blended with the water or added to the other dry ingredients, with the water blended in afterwards.

THE COOKING PROPERTIES OF EGGS

The physical qualities of egg white and yolk make cooking with eggs complex, fascinating and varied. The different properties of the white and yolk during cooking and preparation produce a diverse range of dishes, from light and airy soufflés and sponges to creamy custards and sauces, crisp batters, and rich mayonnaise.

The features that make eggs such a versatile ingredient are their ability to aerate, coagulate and emulsify or, in simpler terms, their ability to foam, set and thicken.

AERATION

When an egg white is beaten or whisked vigorously, air is trapped within the whites, creating a foam. The slightly gelatinous consistency of egg white makes it ideal for trapping and holding bubbles of air. The more vigorously the whites are beaten, the more air will be trapped, stretching the proteins in the egg white and increasing their bulk six to eight times.

The texture of the foam is affected by the size of the bubbles trapped in the white. Larger bubbles will create a softer, wetter foam, whereas small bubbles create a stiffer, drier foam. The longer the white is whisked, the smaller the bubbles will become. Egg whites become over-whisked when the proteins can stretch no further, creating a very dry, crumbly foam. If you continue to whisk past this point, the whites will eventually break down.

For the best results, egg whites should be brought to room temperature by removing them from the refrigerator 20–30 minutes before whisking. If an egg is very cold, its white will become more gelatinous, which can affect its ability to incorporate air. Similarly, very young whites have not developed their full elasticity, causing the same problems, while old whites are often too thin and weak to hold the air or their shape. To ensure good results, add a little cream of tartar to egg whites.

Even a little fat will prevent egg whites from whisking to a foam, so it is vital to use a spotlessly clean, grease-free bowl. Egg yolks also contain fat, so it is very important not to drop any into the whites when separating them.

COAGULATION

When an egg is heated, its proteins change from a liquid form to a semi-solid mass, causing the egg to set. This coagulation occurs at a fairly low temperature of 63°C/145°F. This is a vital aspect of successful egg cooking. For example, if meringues are cooked at too high a temperature, they will burn or brown too much before they have fully dried and hardened, whereas if the temperature is too low, the proteins in the egg whites will not set and the sugar will slowly weep out, leaving a sticky mixture on the tray.

Egg yolks contain a higher proportion of protein than egg whites and therefore react even more sensitively to heat.

Because of this, yolks need careful handling when they are cooked to prevent curdling, which occurs when the protein and liquid separate.

To prevent curdling, cornflour (cornstarch) can be added to stabilize mixtures. This will hold the protein and the liquids together when they are heated and stop them from separating. Many people "cheat" when they make egg custards and pastry sauces by adding cornflour to the mixture. This bypasses the very slow cooking process that would otherwise be necessary.

EMULSION

When a liquid, such as oil, is beaten into an egg, tiny droplets are dispersed evenly throughout the egg, creating a stable mixture. To make a successful emulsion, it is important to use the correct proportion of liquid to egg, otherwise the mixture may not combine properly and is likely to separate. The liquid needs to be beaten into the egg very gradually to allow the egg time to incorporate the liquid. Adding it too quickly is likely to make the mixture separate and curdle.

Classic sauces that rely on the emulsion of egg with another liquid include mayonnaise and hollandaise sauce. Hollandaise sauce relies on heat as well, which melts the butter and allows it to be whisked into the egg. The heat also cooks the yolks very gently, helping the sauce to thicken as the protein in the yolk cooks.

Above: The consistency of egg white is excellent for trapping bubbles of air.

Above: Heat causes the proteins in an egg to solidify.

Above: Oil can be beaten into egg yolk to form an emulsion.

EQUIPMENT

Using the right equipment makes any job easier and usually gives superior results, and this is also true for egg cooking. A good whisk will whip up egg whites to new heights and the best pancake pan will allow batter to be set into thin, even crêpes that can be flipped over or tossed with ease.

There is a huge range of cooking utensils available and you may never need most of them, so consider major purchases carefully to make sure they will be useful in your type of cooking: there are lots of small gadgets that are unnecessary for some cooks, but invaluable to others. An egg separator is a good example, as it is a waste of time for experienced chefs who slip yolks from whites in seconds, but very useful for less confident cooks who fret over broken egg shells and traces of yolk in the white.

Baskets

Wire and wicker egg baskets look attractive and stylish in a kitchen and can be used for storing eggs. They should only be used if you are going to use the eggs quickly. Baskets containing eggs should be kept in a cool, airy room or larder at, or below, a temperature of 20°C/68°F. Do not store them in a musty or windowless room.

Above: Wire baskets are often lantern- or hen-shaped.

Left: Wicker baskets are useful for collecting fresh eggs if you keep a few of your own hens.

Below: Egg timers are very useful when cooking eggs.

a convenient gadget that pierces the egg simply and efficiently without the risk of breaking the egg. The blunt end of the egg is held gently on the concave surface of the piercer and a pin is pressed through the base of the egg when the button is depressed.

Egg separator

Although eggs can be separated by hand, it takes practice. It is crucial in many recipes, such as meringues, to avoid even the slightest drop of yolk in the whites. A metal egg separator separates the yolk and white easily. The separator is placed on the edge of a small bowl and the whole egg is cracked into it. The yolk drops into the middle of the separator and the white falls through the surrounding slits into the bowl.

Wooden spoons and spatulas

These come in a variety of shapes and those shown here are the most useful for cooking with eggs. The smallest spoon is ideal for making small quantities of egg sauces or scrambled egg, the traditional larger spoon is useful for making sauces and creaming cake mixtures. A spatula with holes is good for beating eggs, while one with slits is ideal for lifting poached and fried eggs from the pan. A large flat spatula will produce chunky scrambled egg and is useful for scraping ingredients from the base of a pan.

Egg spoons

These unique implements have three jobs. They can be used to separate the yolk from the white and to beat eggs lightly, and the metal piercer at the end of the handle can be used to pierce the blunt end of eggs before boiling.

Timers

A timer is useful for all sorts of cooking, especially when preparing delicate foods such as eggs. A large timer with a rotating dial is good for longer cooking times, but not so accurate for shorter ones. The flat red timer above is specifically designed for eggs: put it in the pan at the same time as the eggs and it highlights the words that indicate soft, medium or hard cooking stages. The classic egg timer contains a precise amount of sand or salt sealed into an hourglass-shaped container. The grains takes 3 minutes to pass from the top section to the bottom – the time taken to cook a soft-boiled (soft-cooked) egg.

Egg piercer

The blunt end of an egg can be pierced before boiling to allow the expanding air in the air sac to escape. Failing to pierce the egg can cause the shell to crack during cooking. An egg piercer is

Above: Egg separator

Left: A special egg spoon can be used to separate, beat and pierce eggs.

Left: An egg piercer will pierce an egg quickly and easily.

Above: Wooden spoons and spatulas come in all shapes and sizes and are useful for preparing and cooking eggs.

Whisks

There is a selection of sizes and styles of whisk available to suit all tasks.

Wooden and straw whisks can be used to lightly mix ingredients, such as eggs and sauces, but they will not break down lumps or whisk egg whites.

Balloon whisks are shaped like elongated balloons and trap large amounts of air when used properly. The technique is to relax the wrist and rotate the hand. Using the arm can be hard work and does not give the same result. Many experienced cooks and chefs like to roll the balloon whisk back and forth upright between the palms of the hands, working very fast – a method that can be perfected with practice. Although this is ideal when using a small bowl or narrow container, it does not give the maximum volume.

Above from left to right: A small round whisk, a flat whisk, a conical whisk, a long-handled swirled whisk and a rotary whisk are all useful when preparing and cooking eggs.

Small round whisks are useful for mixing small quantities or egg yolks or whites.

Flat whisks give a good airy result when whisking egg whites, but it can take a long time to achieve a very stiff result.

Conical, floppy whisks are useful for sauces and custards.

Long-handled swirled whisks can be used in tall glasses or jugs where there is limited space. They are used in the same way as a balloon whisk.

Rotary whisks, with a pair of beaters, are the best alternative to a hand-held electric beater and are useful for whisking small quantities. They also allow more control than an electric beater.

Right: Balloon whisks come in all sizes, for different tasks, from whisking a spoonful of delicate sauce to whipping up a huge bowl of meringue.

Left: A wooden whisk is best suited to lightly mixing sauces or eggs.

Slotted spoons and spatulas

Large slotted spoons and spatulas are essential for removing eggs from the pan after cooking. Boiled, fried or poached eggs have to be lifted carefully allowing fat or water to drain off before they are transferred to a serving dish. Delicately cooked eggs, such as omelettes, also need to be supported as they are lifted from the pan. Although these tools all perform a similar task, larger rounded spoons are best for fragile poached eggs as they help to keep the egg in a neat shape. Flat, fine-edged spatulas are better for lifting fried eggs or set omelettes or for cutting them into wedges.

UTENSILS FOR COOKING EGGS

Egg poaching pan

Although this is called a poaching pan, it is actually a steamer. The eggs are cooked in individual cups, in a rack over simmering water. The cups have to be greased and a small amount of butter is often used. The result is a cup-shaped egg. The whites can be soft or firm depending on the cooking time; if the water boils too rapidly or for too long, the white can be overcooked and rubbery. One-, two-, and four-egg pans are available.

Above: Slotted spoons and spatulas are good for lifting eggs from a pan.

Egg poaching rings

These rings are designed to keep eggs in a neat shape while they poach. Because the rings prevent the eggs from spreading, it also means that three or four eggs can easily be cooked at the same time.

Above: Poaching rings

Egg coddlers

Coddling is a method of gently cooking eggs in water which had been brought to the boil, then set aside to cool. The whole eggs are placed in the water for about 10 minutes, allowing them to set slowly and very softly. Special coddlers are containers into which the eggs can be broken, rather than leaving them in their shells. The coddlers are placed in gently simmering water. The heat must be kept low to prevent the eggs cooking too firmly around the edges. Coddlers come in two sizes, for medium (US large) eggs and large (US X large) eggs.

Above: Eggs can be steamed in a poaching pan.

Above: Egg coddlers are used to cook eggs very gently.

Below: Heavy omelette pans allow an even spread of heat.

Below: A gently curved non-stick omelette pan helps the omelette to slide easily on to the plate.

Omelette pan

For the best results buy a pan specifically for making omelettes and do not use it for anything else. An omelette pan should be made of aluminium, steel or cast iron and have a thick base throughout, which spreads the heat evenly. It should also have gently curving sides so that the omelette slides out easily on to a plate. A steel pan needs to be seasoned by heating it with oil to prevent sticking and should be wiped clean with kitchen paper, not washed with soap and water.

Pancake pan

A pancake pan should be light with low sides that allow the pancake to be tossed easily. Steel is often used for these pans, but there are also good lightweight non-stick pancake pans. A steel pan needs seasoning and wiping clean to prevent the pancakes from sticking. To season, slowly heat a little oil in the pan until it begins to smoke. Rub the inside of the pan with kitchen paper, then rinse and dry thoroughly.

Above and left: Pancake pans help to produce thin, even pancakes.

Gratin dishes

These shallow ovenproof dishes, available in various sizes, are ideal for baked eggs with added ingredients, such as cream, vegetables or spiced sausage. They can also hold gratinéed fruits or other foods topped with a sabayon sauce, which are then browned in the oven or under the grill (broiler).

Ramekins

These are like miniature soufflé dishes and are usually straight-sided and deep. Ramekins are used for individual portions, such as savoury or sweet mousses, baked eggs and custards. The food may be served in the dish or the dish can act as a mould from which the food is turned out for serving. When cooking delicate dishes, such as custards, ramekins are usually placed in a *bain-marie*, a roasting tin into which water is poured; this protects the mixture from overcooking round the sides of the dish.

Ramekins allow food to cook evenly and their undersides are unglazed, so that the heat penetrates the dish quickly. They are available in white porcelain, ovenproof glass, pottery and many modern china designs that match tableware. The thicker the ramekin, the slower the cooking. Remember that thick ramekins retain heat and food will carry on cooking for some time after it is removed from the oven.

OVENPROOF DISHES

Soufflé dishes

A soufflé dish is characterized by its straight sides. This helps a hot soufflé mixture to rise high and straight. It is often better to use a dish that is slightly too small as this will make the soufflé rise higher. These dishes are also used for chilled soufflés. A paper collar can be tied around the dish to support the mixture while it sets. When the collar is removed, the soufflé will stand above the top of the dish. White porcelain dishes are the classic choice.

Above: Gratin dishes are ideal for baking eggs in the oven.

Below: Soufflé dishes are available in a range of sizes, from small individual ones to very large dishes for several people.

Below: Plain white porcelain ramekins are available in a variety of sizes.

Above:
A blender is
great for making
pancake batters.

Food processors

The food processor has revolutionized food preparation. This fast appliance makes light work of mayonnaise, batters, sauces, pastries and certain cake mixtures. Although small quantities can be processed, many food processors are designed to hold larger quantities and these do not process small quantities efficiently. For example, a small amount of mayonnaise is likely to be lost on the side of the bowl. Select a processor with a slow speed or pulse setting for precise control when preparing delicate mixtures, such as hollandaise sauce. Be careful not to over-process foods.

Above: An electric omelette maker will cook delicious omelettes in minutes.

ELECTRICAL APPLIANCES

Blenders

If you enjoy making mayonnaise and pancakes, you will find a blender invaluable.

Single unit blenders, with a jug (pitcher) on top of the machine, are quick and easy to use and the jug can be immersed in water or taken apart for washing.

Hand blenders, with a purpose-built jug, work quickly and easily, but they do not process larger quantities or tough ingredients.

Free-standing electric mixers, with balloon whisk, beater and extra large bowl are good for making cakes or meringues. A stainless steel bowl is an optional extra. These large food mixers are slower than a food processor, so they can be left to whisk, beat or mix while you work on another part of the recipe. Larger mixers come with a range of optional attachments, including a blender.

Electric omelette makers

An electric omelette maker can cook two small omelettes in a couple of minutes. The heated cooking hollows are brushed with oil or butter to help browning. Any filling is cooked first, then the beaten egg mixture is poured into the hollow, and the lid closed to cook the omelette.

Left: A large, free-standing mixer has a range of useful attachments.

MICROWAVE EGG GADGETS

For those who enjoy microwave cooking, there are several gadgets available that are specifically designed for cooking eggs. The gadgets are essential for some techniques, such as boiling. It is not possible to boil an egg in a microwave as the unpunctured shell is likely to burst. A special microwave egg boiler has hollows for holding the eggs and a lid. The pot of eggs is placed inside the lidded container, with a little water in the base. This allows the eggs to be cooked safely, without the fear of them bursting.

UTENSILS FOR SERVING EGGS

As well as specialist equipment for cooking, there are also a number of utensils that can be useful for serving cooked eggs.

Above: An egg slicer will cut thin, even slices.

Above, clockwise from top right: Special microwave gadgets include an omelette dish, egg coddlers, four- and two-egg poaching dishes and a boiling dish.

Egg slicer

Eggs can be difficult to slice neatly. If you make lots of egg sandwiches, or want neat slices as a garnish, a slicer is invaluable. The cold hard-boiled (hard-cooked) egg is placed in the hollow and then the frame of wires is gently pulled down to cut the egg into neat slices.

Above: An egg cutter will cut the top off a boiled egg neatly and cleanly.

Egg cutters

These round-bladed, deeply serrated scissors are designed for cutting the tops off boiled eggs or at least cracking the top of the shell, ready for a spoon to be used to slip off the top of the egg.

Egg cups

These are essential for holding the awkward-shaped boiled egg steady so that it can be opened and eaten with a spoon. Choice is personal, depending on design and colour. Some egg cups have lids to keep the eggs hot until they are taken to the table.

Left: Egg cups are ideal for holding hot boiled eggs steady and are available in a variety of shapes and sizes.

PREPARATION AND COOKING TECHNIQUES

The joy of cooking with eggs lies in both their simplicity and their versatility. This chapter guides you through all the key techniques that are essential for the successful preparation and cooking of eggs. From the most basic boiling to more complicated advice on making soufflés, roulades and meringues, the range of techniques proves the true versatility of the egg as a cooking ingredient.

Basic Cooking Techniques

Eggs are easy to cook and incredibly versatile, adapting well to a wide variety of cooking techniques. Understanding what happens to an egg when it is heated and cooked helps to make sense of cooking techniques and methods using eggs. Made up of white (albumen) and yolk, an egg consists of mainly water, fat and protein, with smaller proportions of other elements and nutrients. The white is mainly water with protein; the yolk contains fat, protein and other nutrients.

In terms of basic cooking techniques, the protein in an egg makes the most impact: when heated it becomes firm. The longer it is heated, or the hotter the temperature, the firmer it becomes. If an egg is heated too fiercely or for too long, the protein sets too firmly for good eating, which is why overcooked eggs become tough.

When beaten, the proteins from the white combine with those in the yolk and will set at a slightly higher temperature. Instead of the firm white and soft yolk of boiled or fried eggs, beaten eggs can be cooked gently until creamy in texture, as when scrambled or made into an omelette. Cooked over too high a heat, or for too long, scrambled eggs curdle when the protein sets hard and separates leaving a watery residue.

Controlling the heat and length of cooking is the key to cooking eggs successfully. Generally, when making plain cooked eggs, the temperature should not be too high: "very hot" is "too hot". There are exceptions, for example when frying eggs or making an omelette, but in both these cases the high temperature is balanced by very brief cooking, ensuring that the egg does not have time to become tough.

SEPARATING EGGS

When cracking eggs, especially if you intend separating the yolk from the white, make a neat crack around the middle of the shell. Have two bowls ready and, as soon as the shell is cracked, lift the egg, holding both halves together, to stop the yolk from falling into the bowl.

1 To crack the egg, using a single, sharp movement, tap the egg firmly on the side of the bowl as near to the middle of the shell as possible. Alternatively, make an indent in the shell by tapping the egg with the blade of a knife.

2 Use your thumbs to prise the shell halves apart gently, trying to break the shell as little as you possibly can. Turn the shell half containing the yolk upright and let the white from both halves drop into the bowl below.

3 Tilt the shell halves to slip the yolk from one to the other, being careful not to break the yolk. Let the excess white fall into the bowl. Repeat until most of the white has been transferred to the bowl. Slip the yolk into the second bowl and check that there is no more white left in either of the shells.

PIERCING EGGS

Very fresh or cold eggs may crack when placed in boiling water. Although it does not affect the flavour or texture of the egg, it can leave unattractive lumps of cooked white on the outside of the shell. To help prevent the shell from cracking during cooking, pierce the rounded end of the egg, which contains an air space. This allows the expanding air to escape without cracking the shell.

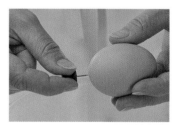

Use a pin to make a small hole in the shell. Pierce the shell gently, by rotating the pin to "drill" a hole. Do not press too hard as this could crack the shell.

Alternatively, use a specially designed egg piercer to make a hole in the shell. Once pierced, immerse the egg in hot water and bring back to the boil.

BOILING EGGS

Eggs should never be boiled rapidly as this is too fast and fierce, frequently causing the shells to crack and resulting in whites with a very rubbery texture. Although eggs can be added to cold water, timing is more accurate when they are added to water that is simmering steadily or boiling gently. Start timing the cooking when the water is bubbling gently again. When boiling soft-boiled (soft-cooked) eggs for further cooking with other ingredients, cook them for fractionally less time than recommended, then plunge them straight into cold water. When cooking hard-boiled (hard-cooked) eggs for salads and garnishes, turn or stir the eggs gently once or twice in the first minute of cooking so that the yolks stay in the middle, then they will look neat when sliced or cut. Freshly laid eggs should be kept for 2–3 days if they are to be hard boiled, otherwise they are difficult to shell.

Simmering and Boiling Eggs

Water simmers when it is on the verge of boiling. Usually, it is brought to the boil first, then the heat is reduced and regulated to keep the water moving gently, with the occasional bubble breaking the surface. When the water only just moves, it is simmering gently; when bubbles regularly break the surface, it is simmering steadily. It is possible to boil water gently, so that bubbles break the surface lightly, instead of boiling rapidly, when bubbles break rapidly and constantly.

Making Perfect Boiled Eggs

1 When cooking chilled eggs until firm, it is best to put them into cold water.

2 Alternatively, lower the eggs on a spoon into simmering water, taking care not to let them drop on to the base of the pan or they will crack.

3 Heat the water until bubbling gently, then begin timing the cooking, using the table below.

Cooking times

This is a guide to cooking eggs added to hot water. Start timing the cooking when the water boils gently. The timings for cooking eggs that are added to cold water are very similar to those for hot water. Just increase cooking time by about 30 seconds. Times can also vary if the eggs are very cold, very fresh or very old. Allow an extra 30 seconds for really fresh eggs (less than 48 hours old) and more if they are very cold.

	Cooking time in minutes		
UK	Small	Medium	Large
US	Med.	Large	X large
Soft	3	4	4½–5
Semi-firm	4	5–6	6–7
(yolks still soft)			
Hard	7	8–10	10–12

SHELLING AND SERVING BOILED EGGS

Soft-boiled (soft-cooked) eggs should be eaten immediately. If they have to stand for 1–2 minutes, crack their tops lightly with the back of spoon or an egg cutter to allow steam to escape and prevent the eggs from cooking further. If they are to be used in other dishes, they should be peeled as soon as they are cool enough to handle.

Eggs are easier to shell when completely cold, so plunge them into cold water immediately after cooking and change the water several times to keep it cold. To prevent black rings from forming around the egg yolks, crack the shells all over with the back of a spoon as soon as the eggs are cooked, and cool the eggs as quickly as possible by placing them in a bowl of cold water. If shelled eggs are not used immediately, store them in cold water in the refrigerator.

How to Serve a Boiled Egg

Use an egg cutter to make a slight crack all around the shell so that the top can be removed easily with a spoon.

Alternatively, cut off the top with a small sharp knife. Tap the shell firmly and evenly with the blade to prevent too much shell from crumbling.

How to Shell a Boiled Egg

1 As soon as the egg is cooked, remove it from the pan and place in a bowl of very cold water. When it has cooled enough to handle, crack the egg shell evenly all over with a teaspoon or tap it gently on a work surface.

2 Start peeling off the shell at the rounded end, where there should be a gap under the shell from the air sac. Lift off the shell and its underlying membrane together, then the shell will peel off easily in large segments. If the shell does not come away from the egg easily, hold it under cold running water for a few seconds.

Eggs for garnishing

Hard-boiled (hard-cooked) egg can be used for garnishes. The eggs should look attractive and appetizing, so take care to cook them perfectly, crack them immediately and cool them quickly. Make sure that they cool completely before cutting.

Using an egg slicer

To cut thin, even slices, use an egg slicer. For the best results use cold, hard-boiled eggs and lightly oil the wires so that they slip through the egg white without breaking it.

Chopping hard-boiled eggs

Use a large knife with a lightly oiled blade to halve or quarter the egg, then chop coarsely or finely, as required. Finely chopped hard-boiled egg can be used to garnish salads or dishes such as savoury mousses or foods set in aspic. Chopped egg can also be used on open sandwiches.

Sieving hard-boiled eggs

Press the yolk and white separately through a fine sieve and use one or both to garnish cold poached fish, dressed crab, savoury mousses and cold soups. Sieved egg can also be used to garnish egg mayonnaise or stuffed eggs.

1 Cooked egg yolk is very soft and is therefore easy to press through a fine sieve, and can be sieved on to a board, directly into salads, or over vegetables or soups.

2 Cooked egg white has a slightly firmer consistency than yolk and will need to be pressed through the sieve quite hard, using the back of a spoon. It is usually easier to press the egg white through the sieve on to a board or into a bowl, rather than directly on to the dish to be garnished. The sieved egg white can then be sprinkled on to the dish.

Stuffing eggs

Hard-boiled (hard-cooked) eggs can be stuffed with many different fillings. Scoop out the yolks from halved hard-boiled eggs, then mash them with the chosen filling ingredients. These eggs are perfect for parties because they can be prepared in advance, then chilled until required.

1 Soft-textured fillings, such as a herb and garlic mixture, cream cheese or flavoured mayonnaise can be spooned into the hollows in the whites using 2 teaspoons.

2 Smooth but firm mixtures, such as this paste made from the egg yolk, tomato, chilli and anchovy essence, can be piped back into the egg whites from a piping (icing) bag fitted with a fairly large nozzle. Use a swirling motion to give an attractive finish.

POACHING EGGS

This simple cooking method still provokes debate about whether to add salt or vinegar, make the water swirl, causing the egg white to wrap itself around the yolk, or add the egg and turn off the heat. All are successful in their own way, but adding salt does encourage the egg to spread. It is important to use really fresh eggs, otherwise the whites spread into wisps.

A poaching ring can help keep the egg in shape. A poaching pan can also be used but gives a slightly different result: the whites tend to be firmer and the egg is saucer-shaped and similar to a soft-boiled (soft-cooked) egg.

Making Classic Poached Eggs

1 Pour about 2.5–4cm/1–1½in water into a frying pan. Add 15ml/1 tbsp vinegar and bring to the boil. Reduce the heat, if necessary, to keep the water bubbling gently. Crack the egg into a cup or small dish so that you can control its position easily when adding it to the pan, then gently tip it into the bubbling water.

2 Cook the egg very gently for 1 minute undisturbed. Then gently spoon a little water over the centre of the egg to cook the yolk.

3 The egg is cooked when it can be loosened easily from the base of the pan. Use a skimmer, slotted spoon or spatula to lift the egg from the water.

4 Trim off any rough edges, using a pair of kitchen scissors. Allow any water to run off the egg and pat dry with kitchen paper before transferring it to a plate or serving dish.

Using a Poaching Ring

To use a poaching ring, place a lightly oiled ring in a pan of gently bubbling water and slide an egg into the ring from a cup. Cook for 1 minute until the white begins to set round the edge. Spoon over boiling water and cook for a further 1–2 minutes, until the top is set. Run a knife around the inside of the ring, lift the egg and ring out of the pan and remove the ring. Drain and serve.

Steam-poaching Eggs

Eggs can be steamed in a poaching pan. A tray of poaching cups holds the eggs out of the simmering water. Partly fill the pan with water and bring to a gentle boil. Add a knob (pat) of butter to each of the individual cups and, when the butter has melted, tip an egg into each one. Cover the pan with a lid and cook for 3 minutes until the top of the egg is just firm. To serve, loosen the egg gently with a round-ended knife and slide on to hot buttered toast.

CODDLING EGGS

This is a very gentle cooking method, giving delicate results. Add the eggs to the pan as for boiling and bring the water to a gentle boil, then cover the pan and remove it from the heat. Leave the eggs to stand for 5–6 minutes for a soft-boiled egg or 7–8 minutes for a firmer set. This cooks the eggs evenly.

Using an Egg Coddler

To use an egg coddler, butter the dish and crack an egg into it. Sprinkle with salt and pepper, replace the lid and place in a pan to simmer for 6–10 minutes, depending on the size of egg used. For a very soft result, turn off the heat and leave to stand for several minutes. Serve the egg in the dish.

BAKING EGGS

Oven-baked eggs in ramekins are delicate, and quick and easy to prepare. They can be flavoured or enriched with a variety of ingredients, such as cream, garlic, ham or cheese, to make delicious appetizers or light meals. Cover the eggs with foil to prevent the yolks from overcooking.

1 Preheat the oven to 180°C/350°F/ Gas 4. Lightly butter the ramekins and crack an egg into each. Top with a knob (pat) of butter and a little seasoning.

2 Stand the ramekins in a roasting tin (pan), half filled with hot water. Bake for 15–18 minutes, until the whites are set.

SCRAMBLING EGGS

These were originally called buttered eggs. Beaten eggs are gently stirred in hot butter over heat until they set. They can be soft and creamy or cooked until quite firm and dry. Water or milk can also be added.

Ingredients can be added to turn plain scrambled eggs into a variety of quick light supper dishes or sandwich fillings. Chopped fresh ingredients such as herbs, diced cooked ham, chopped tomatoes, sliced mushrooms and crushed garlic all go well with scrambled eggs. Store-cupboard (pantry) ingredients, such as anchovy fillets, tuna, frozen peas or canned beans, can also be used.

Scrambled eggs are usually served on toast, but there are many other ways to serve them. Try them on toasted muffins, crumpets or pitta bread. Serve scrambled eggs in baked potatoes or with small pasta shapes, or add them to a bed of cooked spinach.

Making Scrambled Eggs

1 Lightly beat the eggs with seasoning to taste. Allow 3 eggs per person. Heat about 15g/½oz/1 tbsp butter in a small pan until sizzling. Quickly pour in the eggs and stir.

2 Stir the egg mixture frequently over a medium heat for 1–2 minutes, until the eggs are lightly set but still very moist and creamy.

3 For more firmly set scrambled egg, with a slightly drier texture, do not stir quite so frequently and cook for about 4 minutes.

4 If you prefer scrambled eggs with a chunkier texture, use a flat-ended wooden spoon or spatula and stir only occasionally, turning over larger flakes of egg every time.

FRYING EGGS

Eggs can be shallow-fried or deep-fried. Shallow frying with little or no oil is the healthier method, but when deep-fried briefly and well drained, eggs are wonderfully crisp. For both methods the eggs should be very fresh. Fresh light vegetable oil is usually used but a knob (pat) of butter can be added when shallow frying. The fat must be hot enough for the eggs to bubble and cook as soon as they are added to the pan, but not so hot that they break up.

Shallow Frying Eggs

1 Heat 30–45ml/2–3 tbsp oil in a heavy frying pan over a medium heat. There is no need to add oil to a non-stick pan. Crack the egg into the pan and allow it to settle and start bubbling gently around the edges before basting or adding another egg.

2 After 1 minute, spoon a little hot oil over the yolk to cook the egg evenly.

3 Cook for a further 1 minute, until the white has become completely opaque and the edges are just turning brown. If you prefer a firmer yolk, cook the egg for a further minute. Use a spatula to lift the egg out of the pan, carefully allowing oil to drain off for a few seconds or, alternatively, place briefly on a piece of kitchen paper.

4 Alternatively, if you prefer a firmer, crisper egg still, gently flip the egg over, using a fish slice, and cook for a further minute.

Fried eggs in butter sauce
1 Melt 15ml/1 tbsp butter until it begins to foam. Break an egg into the hot butter and cook for about 1 minute until it begins to set.

2 Carefully turn the egg over using a wide spatula that will support the yolk and as much of the white as possible.

3 Cook for a few more seconds until the white around the yolk has set, then remove from the heat. Slide the egg on to a warmed plate to keep warm.

4 To make the sauce, return the pan to the heat and melt about 15ml/1 tbsp butter until it foams. Add a dash of balsamic vinegar and cook for a few more seconds. Pour over the egg and serve.

Deep-frying Eggs

1 Crack the egg into a cup or small bowl so that you can slip it quickly and easily into the pan without splashing yourself with hot oil.

2 Heat about 2.5cm/1in vegetable or sunflower oil in a deep frying pan to 180°C/350°F or until it is hot enough to turn a cube of day-old bread brown in about 45 seconds. Gently slip the egg into the hot oil.

3 Cook the egg for 30 seconds, then use a slotted spoon to turn or fold it over carefully.

4 Cook for a further 30 seconds or until the egg white is crisp and golden on both sides. Use the slotted spoon to remove the egg and drain it on kitchen paper before serving.

BASIC METHODS AND MIXTURES

The magic of cooking with eggs unfolds when they are combined with other ingredients in simple mixtures. These basic methods and mixtures form the basis for the incredible array of dishes that rely on eggs for their success.

Beating and whisking changes the way eggs behave during cooking. Simply beating the white with the yolk creates a mixture that looks quite different from a basic egg; add sugar to this and the mixture will become thick, light and creamy on further beating. When an egg white is whisked it traps a large amount of air, becomes foamy and will stand up in peaks. Being able to trap air in eggs and egg mixtures gives the cook access to a range of methods for both savoury and sweet dishes that will achieve wonderfully varied results.

When mixtures containing eggs are heated, the basic principle of setting, or the protein becoming firm, is true. However, when eggs are combined with air and other ingredients their taste and texture can be very different from that of a whole cooked egg. The following methods and mixtures show how eggs can act as raising agents and lighten other ingredients as well as helping them to set.

BATTERS

A batter is usually a mixture made of flour and a liquid such as milk. Egg is added to the majority of batters. Mixed to different consistencies, a basic flour, egg and milk batter can be used to make any number of wonderful dishes: thin French crêpes, large pancakes or small, thick drop scones (Scotch pancakes or breakfast pancakes) and baked specialities, such as Yorkshire pudding and a French batter pudding called *clafoutis*. With additional raising agents, batters are used for waffles, crumpets and blinis (yeasted buckwheat pancakes). Batters for some dishes, such as pancakes, are allowed to rest after mixing so that the air bubbles subside. When a batter is left to rest, it should be kept cold and covered. If there is any delay before cooking the batter, or you have any left over, it should be chilled.

Making Batter

1 Beat 2 eggs well with an electric beater or by hand.

2 Start to beat in 125g/4oz/1 cup flour until the mixture is too thick to continue. There is no need to sift the flour as any lumps will be beaten out.

3 Add a little milk and the remaining flour and beat to a paste. Gradually add 250ml/8fl oz/1 cup milk and beat until smooth. Set aside for 20 minutes.

4 To make the batter in a blender or food processor, process the flour, egg and a little milk to a paste, then add the remaining milk and process until smooth.

Variations on Basic Batter

Batter can be made with other liquids, such as water, stock or wine. Fizzy beer or cider can be used to lighten batters.

Batter can be flavoured with 15–30ml/ 1–2 tbsp chopped herbs, garlic, mustard, grated citrus rind or a little sugar.

Making Little Yorkshire Puddings

1 Preheat the oven to 220°C/425°F/ Gas 7 for large puddings or 230°C/ 450°F/Gas 8 for small puddings.

2 Place a little fat in the tin (pan) and heat in the oven for 5 minutes until hot.

3 Pour in the batter – the fat should sizzle at once. Bake for 25–30 minutes, reducing the heat to 180°C/350°F/ Gas 4 halfway through cooking time for smaller items.

Making Pancakes

Pancakes are cooked individually, so layer them between sheets of kitchen paper and keep warm in the oven while you cook the remaining batter.

1 Heat a little oil in a pancake pan or frying pan. Pour in a little batter, made with an extra egg. As you do so, tilt and swirl the pan to coat the base with a thin, even layer of batter.

2 Cook over a medium heat until golden underneath. To toss, loosen the edges then slide the pancake to the pan's rim.

3 Jerk the pan upwards, then hold it in the same place to catch the pancake. Alternatively, turn it with a spatula.

4 Cook until the second side is golden, then slide out on to kitchen paper.

Drop Scones

MAKES 18

INGREDIENTS
   225g/8oz/2 cups self-raising
    (self-rising) flour
   2.5ml/½ tsp salt
   15ml/1 tbsp caster (superfine)
    sugar
   1 egg, beaten
   300ml/½ pint/1¼ cups milk
   oil, for cooking

1 Preheat a griddle or heavy frying pan. Sift the flour and salt into a bowl and stir in the sugar. Make a well in the centre.

2 Add the egg and half the milk, then gradually incorporate the flour to make a smooth paste. Gradually beat in the remaining milk until smooth.

3 Lightly oil the griddle or frying pan and drop in tablespoons of batter. Leave until they bubble and the bubbles begin to burst.

4 Turn the drop scones over with a spatula and cook them until the undersides are golden brown. Keep the cooked drop scones warm and moist by wrapping them in a clean napkin while cooking successive batches.

OMELETTES

Lightly beaten eggs, seasoned and fried to form a light omelette provides a meal in about 3 minutes. Any number of seasonings, fillings or toppings can be added to make an omelette more substantial. Thick, set omelettes can be served cold, cut into small portions to make finger food. When the whites are whisked and folded into the yolks, a plain omelette is elevated to soufflé omelette status. With a rich fruit filling, soufflé omelettes make luxurious, yet light desserts.

Although special omelette pans are available, any heavy, medium non-stick frying pan will do. Prepare flavourings and fillings first. Have a warmed serving plate ready and do not cook the omelette until you are ready to eat it. Traditionally rolled or folded to enclose a sweet or savoury filling, an omelette can also be served flat and topped with any flavouring ingredients.

Making a Classic Omelette

1 Allow 3 eggs per omelette. Lightly beat the eggs with seasonings.

2 Heat 15g/½ oz/1 tbsp butter in an omelette or frying pan until very hot and sizzling, but not smoking or browning. Pour in the eggs, tilting the pan slightly.

3 Cook the eggs for a few seconds until the base has set, then use a fork to push in the sides or stir gently. The idea is to ensure that the unset egg mixture runs on to the hot pan and starts cooking. Cook for about 1 minute or until the egg is just beginning to set. For a firmer set, cook for a little longer.

4 Use a large flat spatula to fold over a third of the omelette.

5 Tilting the pan away from you, flip the omelette over again and slide it out immediately on to a warmed serving plate in one action.

COOK'S TIP

For the perfect omelette, the egg in the middle should still be slightly runny or creamy when served, but the omelette can be completely set if preferred.

Making a Soufflé Omelette

The eggs are separated and the whites whisked until stiff. The whites are then folded into the yolk mixture to give a large volume of light mixture. A savoury or sweet filling may be added to the cooked omelette, which must be served promptly before it collapses.

1 Separate the eggs. Beat the yolks with seasoning or a little sugar in a large bowl. Whisk the whites until stiff, then fold them into the yolks until evenly blended. Preheat the grill (broiler).

2 Heat 15g/½oz/1 tbsp butter in an omelette pan or frying pan and spoon in the mixture, spreading it out evenly.

3 Cook gently for 2–3 minutes, until the mixture is golden and firm underneath and only just firm on top.

4 The omelette can be served as it is or finished under the grill. Hold the pan under the grill for a few seconds, keeping it slightly away from the heat as the omelette will rise. Cook for a few seconds until lightly browned on top.

5 Spoon the chosen filling or fruit conserve over a third of the omelette.

6 Use a large spatula to fold the cooked omelette in half and immediately transfer it to a warm serving plate.

To add the professional-looking skewer marks on top, heat a greased skewer in a gas flame until almost glowing. Then press the skewer gently, but firmly, on the top of the omelette to mark diagonal lines. A sweet omelette can be dredged with icing (confectioners') sugar before being scored in this way.

SET THICK OMELETTES

Instead of folding or topping a lightly cooked thin omelette to incorporate a filling, the ingredients can be set in the beaten egg mixture. For a set thick omelette, a much larger proportion of flavouring ingredients are used, usually vegetables such as potato and onion. The mixture is cooked very slowly until set. The cooked omelette can be served hot, warm or cold, cut into wedges or fingers. Spanish tortilla and Italian frittata are both set omelettes.

Making Spanish Omelette

1 Heat a mixture of butter and oil in a large heavy frying pan, then add sliced potatoes and onions and cook gently until almost tender. Beat 6 eggs with seasoning, a crushed garlic clove and plenty of chopped parsley. Pour the eggs evenly over the hot vegetables. Continue cooking gently for 4–5 minutes or until the egg has almost set.

2 Place a plate over the top of the pan. Put your hand firmly on the top and hold the pan with a cloth, then quickly turn over both pan and plate together.

3 Lift off the pan and allow the omelette to slip out on to the plate.

4 Slide the omelette back into the pan, cooked side up, and continue cooking until set and golden underneath. Serve hot or cool, cut into slices or wedges, with salad as an accompaniment.

Omelette fillings

For a thin folded omelette, try sliced mushrooms, sautéed in a little butter; a sprinkling of grated cheese, such as Cheddar, with chopped parsley; or 1–2 spoonfuls of chopped smoky ham.

Sweet soufflé omelettes are best served with a fruit filling such as a really good conserve, warmed with a splash or two of brandy to help it spread, or try fresh raspberries, flamed in liqueur, with cream.

For a thick set omelette, try adding lightly sautéed spinach or courgette (zucchini), or slices of spicy sausage to the basic potato and onion filling.

USING EGGS FOR BINDING, COATING AND GLAZING

Eggs are perfect for these three tasks. They bind ingredients in burgers, pâtés and similar dishes, ensuring they retain their shape during cooking. Together with flour and breadcrumbs, eggs make a delicate coating for fine foods. They are also used to lighten batters that coat and protect foods during frying. Beaten egg or egg yolk give an attractive golden glaze to many baked items.

Binding with Egg

Eggs can be added to the ingredients for burgers, pâtés, fish cakes, potato cakes, rissoles, meatloaves and similar mixtures. As the mixture cooks, the egg sets and helps to hold the ingredients together. Add 1 egg to every 450g/1lb ingredients.

Simple fish cakes

In a large bowl, mix together 200g/7oz can tuna or salmon with 300g/11oz/2¾ cups mashed potatoes. Season with 30ml/2tbsp chopped fresh parsley or dill, salt and freshly ground black pepper, then mix in 1 beaten egg. Shape the mixture into 8 patties. Dip each pattie in beaten egg, then coat in fine white breadcrumbs.

Grill (broil) the fishcakes on both sides until golden brown. Divide them among 4 warmed plates and serve with steamed courgettes (zucchini).

Coating with Egg and Breadcrumbs

Coating food, such as rissoles, potato cakes and fish and shellfish, with egg and breadcrumbs protects it from fierce heat during frying. Cover the food in flour, then dip in beaten egg and finally coat in fine white breadcrumbs. When cooked, the coating is deliciously crisp and golden and the filling is very moist.

Glazing with Egg

Pastries and breads, particularly savoury items, bake to a rich golden finish when brushed lightly with beaten egg. Whole beaten egg may be used or, for a very rich glossy finish, egg yolk can be lightly beaten with a little water and a pinch of salt or sugar. Beaten egg can also be used to seal the surface of pastry. Brush egg white over the base of a pastry case (shell) to prevent the filling from oozing into the pastry or brush beaten whole egg on pastry edges that need to be sealed together, such as the top and bottom of a pie crust.

SAVOURY EGG SAUCES

Many classic savoury sauces are based on egg, either emulsified with hot butter or a good oil, or cooked slowly with a little liquid and whisked continuously over a gentle heat. The results are wonderfully luscious. Velvet-textured egg and butter hollandaise sauce complements simple grilled (broiled) fish or vegetables, while Béarnaise sauce is perfect for grilled meats.

Patience and a gentle touch are vital when making sauces. Fierce heat and fast cooking or mixing can ruin egg-based mixtures. For the more cautious, cook butter sauces very slowly in a bowl placed over a pan of simmering water – be warned, this does take a very long time. When you are more confident sauces can be made in a small heavy pan over gentle heat.

Making Hollandaise Sauce

1 Whisk 3 large egg yolks in a pan with a few drops of white wine vinegar, 15ml/1 tbsp lemon juice and seasoning.

2 Heat 175g/6oz/¾ cup butter until bubbling. Gradually pour into the egg mixture, whisking continuously over a very gentle heat. Cook slowly, whisking more frequently as the sauce heats. Whisk very fast if any lumps appear.

3 Continue cooking very slowly, stirring or whisking continuously, until the sauce is thick and velvety. Use immediately or keep warm.

4 If the sauce begins to curdle, remove from the heat and transfer to a bowl, then whisk until the sauce cools.

Making Béarnaise Sauce

1 Boil 2 chopped shallots, 1 sliced garlic clove, 4 black peppercorns and a few sprigs of parsley and tarragon in 30ml/2 tbsp water and 60ml/4 tbsp wine vinegar until reduced by half. Beat 3 large (US X large) egg yolks and melt 175g/6oz/¾ cup butter until hot.

2 Strain the hot vinegar and pour on to the egg yolks, whisking continuously. Then whisk in the hot butter and follow steps 2, 3 and 4 for hollandaise sauce.

Keeping butter sauces warm

These hot sauces can be made in advance and kept warm. Cover with clear film and press it on the surface to prevent any air from entering. Place the bowl over a pan of warm water. Alternatively, if the sauce has been covered and left to go cold, it can be reheated gently in the microwave.

Butter sauces can be made a day ahead and chilled or they can even be frozen. Reheat gently, whisking all the time before serving.

MAYONNAISE

Unlike cooked butter sauces, creamy mayonnaise achieves its thick and glossy texture by beating alone. A mild-flavoured oil is gradually beaten into an egg to create a thick emulsion.

Making Mayonnaise

1 Whisk 1 large (US X large) egg in a bowl with 2.5ml/½ tsp French mustard, the juice of ½ lemon or 30ml/2 tbsp white wine vinegar and salt and pepper.

2 Prepare 600ml/1 pint/2½ cups oil: a mixture of good vegetable oil or sunflower oil and light olive oil mixed half and half is suitable.

3 Whisking continuously, slowly pour in the oil in a very fine stream. For a richer mayonnaise, use 2 egg yolks and allow about 300ml/½ pint/1¼ cups olive oil.

4 Keep whisking and adding oil, until the mixture thickens to form a smooth, glossy mayonnaise. A large egg should take most of the oil. Chill until required.

5 Mayonnaise can be stored in the refrigerator in sealed jar for a week.

Making mayonnaise in a food processor or blender
As with butter sauces, time and patience are vital to a successful mayonnaise. However, it can be made quickly and easily in a food processor or blender. Care still needs to be taken when adding the oil because adding it too quickly can cause mayonnaise to separate.

It is best to make larger quantities as small amounts of mayonnaise are lost against the sides of the bowl or jug. Blend together the egg and flavourings. With the machine running, gradually drizzle in the oil, a little at a time, until the mixture thickens to form a glossy mayonnaise.

SWEET EGG SAUCES

Sweet sauces include light and fluffy sabayon, which can be served on its own or as a glaze for grilled (broiled) fruits, and proper custard, a world apart from anything available in a can or packet. All these sauces are easy to make and it is well worth having a go if you are not familiar with them.

Making Custard

1 Heat 450ml/¾ pint/scant 2 cups milk with a few drops of vanilla essence and remove from the heat just as the milk comes to the boil. Whisk 2 eggs and 1 yolk in a bowl with 15–30ml/1–2 tbsp caster (superfine) sugar. Blend together 15ml/1 tbsp cornflour (cornstarch) with 30ml/2 tbsp water and mix with the eggs. Whisk in a little of the hot milk, then mix in all the remaining milk.

2 Strain the egg and milk mixture back into the pan and heat gently, stirring frequently to prevent lumps forming.

3 Continue stirring until the custard thickens sufficiently to coat the back of a wooden spoon. Serve immediately or cover the surface of the sauce with clear film to prevent a skin from forming and keep warm in a heatproof bowl over a pan of hot water.

Making Baked Custard

1 Preheat the oven to 180°C/350°F/ Gas 4. Coat an ovenproof dish with caramel or grease it with a little butter. Arrange a layer of fresh fruit in the base of the dish, if you like.

2 Beat together 4 large (US X large) eggs, a few drops of vanilla essence and 15–30ml/1–2 tbsp caster (superfine) sugar. Whisk in 600ml/1 pint/2½ cups hot milk and then strain the custard into the prepared dish.

3 Stand the dish in a roasting pan and pour in warm water to half fill it. Bake for 50–60 minutes, or until lightly set.

Making Sabayon Sauce

1 Whisk 1 egg yolk and 15ml/1 tbsp caster (superfine) sugar per portion in a large heatproof bowl over a pan of simmering water. Gradually whisk in 30ml/2 tbsp sweet white wine, liqueur or full-flavoured fruit juice, such as cranberry juice.

2 Whisk the sauce continuously over a constant heat until the mixture becomes very frothy.

3 Continue whisking until the sauce is thick enough to hold a trail on top of the mixture. Serve immediately or remove the bowl from the pan and continue whisking until cool.

SOUFFLÉS

A beautifully risen hot soufflé is the star of any dinner, but many highly competent cooks are so nervous about making a hot soufflé that they never even attempt to do so. In fact, hot soufflés are very simple to make and the cook's major concern should not be the soufflé rising on cue (you can always pour another drink while your diners wait), but making sure the guests are sitting ready to appreciate the soufflé's grand entrance. Remember that a soufflé cannot be rushed, have the oven at the right temperature and do not open the door until you are really sure that it is cooked. When the soufflé is put into a hot oven it starts rising immediately but if the oven is not preheated, the mixture will begin to set before it can rise.

Iced and cold soufflés are a grander version of a mousse. They are fluffier, lightened with whisked egg white and set with gelatine, then piled high in a soufflé dish surrounded by a collar of paper to support the mixture and give a "risen" appearance. They can be served well chilled or part-frozen. Cold soufflés are much easier to make than their appearance suggests and they are sure to impress your guests.

Preparing a Soufflé Dish

Some cooks recommend tying a collar around a dish for a hot soufflé, but this is not necessary as the mixture will hold itself up. If you want the soufflé to rise very high, use a smaller dish with a collar, then remove the collar before serving the soufflé. A collar is essential for a cold soufflé. It supports the mixture, which is poured in above the rim of the dish. For a neat finish, and to

avoid having any mixture leaking down between the paper and the dish, the collar must be attached firmly.

Cut a piece of greaseproof (waxed) paper long enough to wrap around the soufflé dish and wide enough to stand at least 7.5cm/3in above the rim of the dish when folded in half. Fold the paper in half, to provide a double thickness and attach one end to the dish with sticky tape. Wrap the paper tightly and evenly around the dish and secure the end with tape. Grease the inside of the paper. If making a hot soufflé, grease the inside of the dish as well.

Making a Baked Soufflé

Most hot soufflés are based on a thick white sauce. Before you begin, grease a soufflé dish and preheat the oven to 200°C/400°F/Gas 6.

1 Melt 25g/1oz/2 tbsp butter in a pan and blend in 25g/1oz/¼ cup plain (all-purpose) flour. Whisk in 300ml/½ pint/1¼ cups warm milk and bring to the boil, whisking until thickened. Remove from the heat, leave to cool slightly and mix in 4 egg yolks.

2 Add the chosen flavouring ingredients, for example paprika, mustard and grated cheese, and stir until evenly mixed.

3 Whisk the egg whites until stiff, but not dry. Beat in a spoonful of the whites to soften the yolk mixture, then fold in the main portion of egg white using a large flat spatula or metal spoon. Cut through and fold over the mixture so that the whites are mixed in evenly.

4 Gently spoon the mixture into the soufflé dish, taking care not to knock out the air. Run your finger around the top edge, just inside the rim to make a narrow channel in the mixture. This will help the soufflé rise evenly.

5 Sprinkle a cheese soufflé with grated Parmesan cheese or fine breadcrumbs. Bake at once for 30–35 minutes. Place the dish low enough down in the oven to allow the soufflé room to rise. Do not open the oven door during cooking as this may cause the soufflé to sink.

Soufflé effects

Give a soufflé a surprise centre by adding an ingredient that needs brief, light cooking, such as fish or cooked vegetables. Try adding chunks of skinned, boned salmon or smoked haddock to a light cheese and herb soufflé. Spoon half the soufflé mixture into the dish. Add the fish and spoon the rest of the mixture over the top. Cook as usual.

To give a soufflé a cracked top or top-hat effect, make a deep cut in the top of the mixture with a spoon or knife.

Making a Cold or Iced Soufflé

1 Prepare a soufflé dish with a collar. Make 450ml/¾ pint/scant 2 cups thick custard and pour into a large bowl. Set aside to cool.

2 Dissolve 15ml/1 tbsp powdered gelatine in 45ml/3tbsp water and blend with the chosen flavouring, such as coffee essence, mocha syrup or sieved crushed fruit, and stir into the custard. Mix well until the flavouring is evenly blended with the custard. Chill.

3 When the mixture is beginning to set, whisk the egg whites with caster (superfine) sugar as for meringue.

4 Fold the meringue into the custard mixture. Use a large balloon whisk for folding in because it will help to break up the meringue more evenly and blend the two textures.

5 When the mixture is nearly set, carefully pour it into the prepared dish or tin. The mixture should come about 5cm/2in above the rim. Chill until set or freeze for at least 1 hour before serving to make an iced soufflé.

6 When ready to serve the soufflé, carefully, and very slowly, peel off the paper collar. If the paper does not come away easily, use a warm, round-bladed knife to start it off.

7 Coat the side of the soufflé with chocolate or chopped toasted nuts. Press the coating on the soufflé using a spatula. Decorate the top with piped cream and/or more chocolate.

Cold Savoury Soufflés

These can be made by the same basic method as a cold sweet soufflé, using a plain savoury sauce or purée of ingredients as the base. Dissolve the gelatine into the flavouring mixture, stir into the savoury sauce, then allow to part-set before folding in the egg whites.

Coating the soufflé dish

To give hot or cold soufflés additional flavour, the inside of the dish can be coated before adding the mixture. Grated chocolate complements a sweet coffee soufflé. For a savoury soufflé, try using grated Parmesan cheese or fine breadcrumbs: plain white breadcrumbs can be used when making a baked soufflé, and toasted breadcrumbs complement a chilled soufflé. Butter the dish, then shake the coating liberally all over the inside. Tip out any excess.

PASTRY

Eggs are often used to enrich pastry. They help to bind the dry ingredients together, make the pastry more pliable and give a rich crumbly result. Whole egg can be used but it is more common to use just the yolk as the white can give a tough result. Eggs are also a key ingredient for choux pastry in which they act as the setting agent and, along with air, help the pastry to rise.

Making Rich Shortcrust Pastry

Rub together 115g/4oz/1 cup butter, margarine or white fat into 225g/8oz/ 2 cups plain (all-purpose) flour. Blend in 1 egg yolk and a little cold water, then mix thoroughly to form a smooth dough. Chill for about 10 minutes.

Making Rich Cheese Pastry

This delicious savoury pastry is perfect for all occasions. It uses cream cheese as well as butter.

Sift 225g/8oz/2 cups plain (all-purpose) flour and a pinch of salt on to a cold work surface or into a large bowl. Add 75g/3oz/6 tbsp each of soft butter and cream cheese and 1–2 egg yolks. Rub together with your fingers, until a thick paste forms. Chill for 10 minutes.

Making Choux Pastry

This pastry is the base for éclairs and profiteroles. It is also used for savoury pastries such as gougère, a filled ring of choux pastry, and aigrettes, which are deep-fried cheese choux buns. When the pastry cooks, it fills with air, creating a hollow that is perfect for filling.

1 Sift 65g/2½oz/9 tbsp plain (all-purpose) flour and a pinch of salt on to a sheet of baking parchment.

2 Melt 50g/2oz/4 tbsp butter in a small pan with 150ml/¼ pint/⅔ cup cold water. Bring to a rolling boil, then remove from the heat.

3 Tip the sifted flour into the pan all at once and beat together quickly to make a stiff paste that comes away from the sides of the pan in a ball. Do not beat hard or the paste will become oily. Leave to cool slightly.

4 Gradually pour 3 beaten eggs into the paste, beating hard to combine after each addition.

5 The mixture will be slightly lumpy at first, but keep beating hard until the egg and paste are thoroughly mixed and have a smooth and glossy texture.

6 If the paste is too firm, add an additional 15–30ml/1–2 tbsp beaten egg to the mixture. It should have a firm dropping consistency.

7 Line a baking sheet with baking parchment or grease it well. To make profiteroles, use two teaspoons to place small quantities of choux paste on the prepared baking sheet, spacing them well apart.

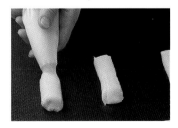

8 To make éclairs, place the paste in a piping (icing) bag without a nozzle and pipe 5cm/2in long cylinders well apart in neat lines.

9 Preheat the oven to 200°C/400°F/ Gas 6. Bake medium-size buns for 20–25 minutes; smaller buns for a few minutes less; éclairs for 30–35 minutes and larger rings for 40–45 minutes.

SAVOURY ROULADES

These are based on the basic savoury soufflé mixture, which is then baked in a Swiss (jelly) roll tin (pan).

Making a Savoury Roulade

1 Grease and lightly dust the tin or line with baking parchment. Preheat the oven to 190°C/375°F/Gas 5.

2 Melt 25g/1oz/2 tbsp butter in a pan and blend in 25g/1oz/¼ cup plain (all-purpose) flour. Whisk in 300ml/½ pint/1¼ cups warm milk and bring to the boil, whisking until thickened. Cool slightly, then beat into 4 egg yolks.

3 Stir in flavouring ingredients, such as well-seasoned spinach purée or cheese.

4 Whisk 4 egg whites stiffly, then fold in the sauce, until evenly blended.

5 Pour the mixture into the prepared tin and spread it evenly into the corners. Bake for 10–12 minutes, or until just firm to the touch. If it is overcooked, the edges become too crisp and the roulade will not roll easily.

6 While the roulade is cooking, lay a sheet of greaseproof (waxed) paper on a clean dishtowel. Sprinkle with finely grated Parmesan cheese, if you wish. Invert the hot roulade on to the paper and leave to cool slightly before removing the lining paper.

7 Savoury mixtures are best rolled up while hot, but they can also be rolled as they cool. Roll up the roulade using the dishtowel and paper as support. Wrap the roulade in the dishtowel to keep it moist until you are ready to unroll it and add the filling.

WHISKED SPONGES

These incredibly light sponges have an open airy texture. They can be plain or flavoured and baked in layers or fingers, or in thin rectangles for making Swiss (jelly) rolls and roulades. Luscious or light fillings can be added after cooking. The sponge can be made without fat, or melted butter can be added, as for Genoese sponge; allow about 15g/½oz/1 tbsp butter per egg. This will give a richer, slightly more dense sponge with better keeping qualities. Fatless sponges become stale very quickly, so are best used on the day they are made; however, they do freeze well. Sponge with added butter will keep in an airtight container for 1–2 days.

Preparing tins

A sponge sandwich tin (pan) or a deep cake tin should be greased and dusted lightly with flour. The thin flour coating provides a surface to which the light mixture clings as it rises and this helps to give a neat straight side on the baked sponge. If you are concerned that the sponge may stick to the base of the tin, then line it with baking parchment after greasing and flouring the sides. This will also help to support the cake when it is turned out.

To prepare a Swiss (jelly) roll tin (pan), cut a sheet of lining paper at least 2.5cm/1in larger than the tin. Stand the tin on the paper and draw around its base. Use scissors to snip into the corners. Place the paper in the tin, overlapping the corners neatly.

Making a Whisked Sponge

Whisking the mixture over hot water helps to make a far lighter sponge.

1 Grease and lightly dust the tin (pan) or line with baking parchment. Preheat the oven to 190°C/375°F/Gas 5.

2 Using an electric beater, whisk the eggs and sugar in a large heatproof bowl over a pan of simmering water.

3 Continue whisking until the mixture is very pale, fluffy and thick. The sponge mixture should hold a trail when you lift out the whisk. Remove the bowl from the heat and continue to whisk until the mixture cools.

4 Sift the flour twice, then fold it into the whisked mixture. Fold in the melted butter, if using.

5 Continue folding very gently with a large spatula until thoroughly mixed. Pour the sponge mixture into the prepared tins. Bake for 10–12 minutes until well risen and springy to touch.

Making a Swiss (Jelly) Roll

These are made from a whisked sponge cooked in a Swiss (jelly) roll tin (pan). The prepared sponge should be rolled up while still warm to prevent cracking.

1 While the sponge is cooking, lay a sheet of greaseproof (waxed) paper on a clean dishtowel. Sprinkle the paper liberally with caster (superfine) sugar.

2 Gently invert the sponge on to the centre of the paper, then slowly peel off the lining paper. If the paper does not come away easily, use a rounded knife to ease the paper from the sponge.

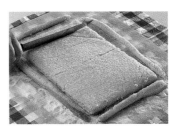

3 Trim the edges using a sharp knife, then make a shallow cut 2.5cm/1in from one short side of the cake to help it begin to roll.

4 Roll up the cake while it is still warm, using the towel as support. Leave the greaseproof paper inside so the sponge does not stick to itself while cooling. Set aside to cool.

5 Carefully unroll the sponge, spread with jam and cream or your chosen filling, then carefully roll up again.

> **Sweet roulades**
> These can be made with other mixtures, such as meringue, but are always cooked in a Swiss (jelly) roll tin (pan).

MERINGUE

Meringues were invented by a Swiss chef from the town of Merhrinyghen who discovered the culinary delights produced by the simple combination of foamy egg whites and fine sugar. This basic mixture is sometimes referred to as Swiss meringue. Some quite wonderful dishes have evolved from these beginnings. The air bubbles incorporated during whisking are crucial to the success of meringue; without them the foamy sugar mixture would not be formed to create these melt-in-the-mouth desserts.

Egg whites should be at room temperature as this allows them to be whisked to maximum volume. Damp or humid conditions are not ideal for meringues as their high sugar content tends to absorb moisture, so try to wait for a warm dry day before making them. Use fresh eggs and very clean, grease-free equipment. A metal or glass bowl will give the best results; copper gives a particularly light result. Avoid plastic, which tends to harbour minute amounts of grease on its surface. The bowl should be as large as possible to allow the maximum air to be whisked in. Whisk slowly at first, then gradually increase the speed to maximum.

Although it is possible to overwhisk egg whites, the more common fault is not whisking them enough, so carry on until they are really stiff. Whisked egg whites for meringues should be stiffer than for most recipes. When whisked for meringue, the whites are referred to as being "dry" because they look almost dry in texture and they can be cut with a knife to leave a clean, flat surface on the foamy white. Try the test at step 3, right, and you will soon know if the whites are at the right consistency.

The usual proportion of ingredients is 25–50g/1–2oz/2–4 tbsp caster (superfine) sugar to each egg white. Cream of tartar, salt, cornflour (cornstarch) and vinegar are sometimes added. Cream of tartar or salt helps to stiffen the whites before the sugar is added. Cornflour and vinegar help to give a meringue with a soft and chewy middle contrasting with a crisp crust.

Making Meringue

A large balloon whisk will give excellent results when whisking meringue. This can be very hard work so it may be preferable to use an electric whisk. However, you will achieve better results if you can whisk in the sugar by hand.

1 Preheat the oven to 150°C/300°F/Gas 2. Stand the bowl on a damp cloth to prevent it from sliding. Whisk the egg whites using a wide sweeping and folding motion. Once the whites have broken down, whisk faster, using a larger motion to incorporate more air.

2 Continue until the whites are standing up in stiff peaks.

3 When the whites are whisked sufficiently, they will not fall out when you turn the bowl upside down.

4 Gradually sprinkle in the caster (superfine) sugar, a few tablespoons at a time, whisking continuously until all the sugar has been added. Continue whisking until the meringue is thick and glossy. It should hold big stiff peaks.

5 Line a baking sheet with non-stick tray liners or baking parchment. To make simple meringues, use two tablespoons to place large spoonfuls of meringue mixture well apart on the prepared baking sheet. Allow the meringue mixture to form neat, rounded shapes (equal in size) with soft peaks.

Drying Meringue

To achieve crisp, white meringues, the mixture needs very slow gentle cooking. This allows the meringue to dry out, without becoming brown. Preheat the oven to 150°C/300°F/Gas 2. Bake the meringue for 10 minutes, then reduce the heat to 140°C/275°F/Gas 1. Allow a further 30–40 minutes for individual meringues and shapes, depending on size. Larger meringues or layers for gâteaux should be dried for at least 1 hour. Thick layers of meringue or a deep pavlova may take 1–2 hours. Turn off the heat and leave the cooked meringue in the cooling oven until cold and crisp.

Poaching Meringue

Individual portions of meringue can be poached, giving a soft, rather than crisp, texture. They are usually poached in milk but a light fruit juice mixture or vanilla-flavoured water can also be used and will give a lighter result.

Use two serving spoons to shape ovals of meringue and carefully drop them into a pan of gently simmering water. Cook for about 1 minute, then turn the meringues and cook for a further minute. Use a slotted spoon to remove the meringues and serve with a hot sauce, fruit or ice cream.

Cooked Meringue

A cooked meringue is made by whisking together the egg whites and sugar in a large bowl over a pan of hot water. This produces a far more stable mixture than uncooked meringue. It will be able to stand for longer without starting to collapse (or seep sugary liquid). Cooked meringue can be dried in the same way as basic meringue.

Cooked meringue can also be used in soufflés and mousses instead of raw egg whites.

Italian Meringue

This type of meringue is made using a similar method to cooked meringue but uses hot sugar syrup instead of sugar. This produces a particularly stable mixture, which is perfect for the cake frosting that this meringue is so often used for.

Unlike uncooked meringue, Italian meringue will not start to separate if left to stand. Instead it will form a slightly dry crust that conceals the soft and gooey frosting underneath.

Making Italian Meringue

1 Dissolve 175g/6oz/¾ cup caster (superfine) sugar in 90ml/6 tbsp water, then bring to the boil. Boil until clear and reduced to a syrup-like consistency. Keep hot. Whisk the egg whites over a pan of simmering water until stiff.

2 Gradually pour the hot syrup into the whites, adding it in a slow, steady trickle and whisking continuously.

3 Continue whisking until the mixture is very stiff and glossy. Remove the bowl from over the pan and continue whisking until the meringue is cool.

Chocolate meringue fingers

MAKES 10–12

INGREDIENTS
2 egg whites
115g/4oz/generous ½ cup caster (superfine) sugar
115g/4oz bitter chocolate

1 Preheat the oven to 150°C/300°F/Gas 2. Lightly oil 2 non-stick baking trays. Whisk the egg whites until stiff and peaky. Gradually whisk in the sugar until the mixture is stiff and glossy and will hold in firm peaks.

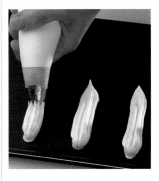

2 Spoon the meringue into a piping (icing) bag with medium-size star nozzle and pipe rows of 5–6cm/2–2½in meringue fingers.

3 Place the trays in the oven for 7 minutes, then reduce the heat to 140°C/275°F/Gas 1 and cook for a further 30 minutes. Turn off the oven and leave to cool.

4 Break the chocolate into a bowl placed over a small pan of simmering water and stir until it has melted, then cool slightly. Dip one or both ends of the meringues into the chocolate, letting the excess drip back into the bowl. Place the fingers on a cooling rack until the chocolate has set.

Piping Meringue

The stiff texture of meringue is perfect for piping. Small meringue rosettes can be used to decorate desserts or serve with fruit; nests can be filled with fruit, flavoured creams or ice cream.

1 Fit a star nozzle in a large piping (icing) bag and fill with meringue. To pipe rosettes, make one swirling motion, then pipe across and around again. Lift up the nozzle sharply to make a peak.

2 To make nests, use a star nozzle and pipe using a swirling motion to make the base. Then pipe a top outer rim to make sides for the nest.

3 To make the base of a meringue gâteau or Vacherin, use a plain or fluted nozzle and pipe a continuous spiral of meringue to form a large round.

4 To top an open tart filled with apple or lemon with meringue, pipe meringue in a neat lattice design.

5 Alternatively, pipe very small rosettes all the way round the edge of an open tart or pie.

Cooking meringue toppings

Any open tart or pie is delicious topped with piped meringue. A sweet, mouthwatering meringue topping complements a slightly sharp filling, such as gooseberries, rhubarb, blackberries or lemon curd, perfectly.

Meringue toppings are quite different from dry meringue and need to be cooked in a different way. They should be cooked at a much higher temperature, to give a crisp light brown outside of caramelized sugar, and a soft mallowy inside.

Start cooking the tart or pie and, when it is nearly cooked, spoon or pipe the meringue over the filling. Return to the oven and cook at 200°C/400°F/Gas 6 for a further 7–8 minutes or until golden brown and crisp.

Making Meringue Rounds

Layers of crunchy meringue sandwiched with fruit and/or cream fillings make a stunning dessert. Toasted nuts give the best flavour. Try hazelnuts or almonds and chop them finely as they give a good crunchy texture superior to that obtained by grinding the nuts finely. Line two or more baking sheets with baking parchment. It helps to draw a circle on the reverse of the paper in heavy pencil, then use it as a guide when spreading the meringue.

1 Fold the toasted nuts evenly and gently into the prepared meringue.

2 Gently spread the nutty meringue mixture evenly into flat circles about 20–22.5cm/8–9in in diameter on the prepared baking sheets.

PAVLOVA

This much-loved dessert is a delicious variation on the meringue theme. Pavlova has a crisp outer layer that conceals a soft and chewy centre. It is usually filled with cream and fresh fruits and makes a luxurious finale to a dinner party.

The dessert is thought to have originated in Australia, created by a chef in Perth. Named after the Russian ballerina Anna Pavlova who visited Australia in 1926, the fluffy meringue sides are thought to represent the ballerina's tutu.

Pavlova is surprisingly easy to make and can be made in advance and stored in an airtight container. Although every cook seems to have their own secret for attaining the prized mallowy centre, there are three main elements during preparation that make pavlova different from other meringues: the addition of cornflour (cornstarch) and vinegar; folding in, rather than whisking in, the sugar and the depth of the cooked meringue. These key differences in the dessert's preparation help to create the softer, chewier centre.

Pavlova fillings

There are a great many variations on the traditional pavlova, though the most authentic fruit filling is thought to be passion fruit. Many combinations of fruits can be used or chopped fruit can be mixed into the whipped cream. The cream can also be flavoured with lemon curd, or a teaspoon of brandy or liqueur can be stirred in at the last minute.

The fruit can be substituted entirely, if wished, and replaced with grated or chipped chocolate or crushed ratafia biscuits (almond macaroons).

The meringue shell can be sprinkled with flaked (sliced) almonds, shredded coconut, cocoa powder or grated chocolate halfway through cooking to add extra flavour and texture.

Making Pavlova

1 Start by making a traditional meringue mixture using 4 egg whites but do not whisk in all of the sugar. Sift 15–30ml/ 1–2 tbsp cornflour (cornstarch) over the meringue, then fold in the last of the sugar. The amount of cornflour depends on the number of egg whites used.

2 Add 15ml/1 tbsp light vinegar such as white wine vinegar or distilled white vinegar.

COOK'S TIP

When filling a pavlova, always make sure that the serving plate is completely flat. The weight of the filling may cause the pavlova to sink into a slightly curved dish, cracking the crisp outer layer of the pavlova beyond repair.

If you do have a disaster when making a pavlova, combine the broken pieces of meringue with cream and fruit and freeze for several hours to make a delicous soft-scoop ice cream.

3 Use a large metal spoon or plastic spatula to cut through the mixture and fold it over, incorporating the vinegar until evenly blended. Work very gently to avoid knocking out any of the air from the meringue.

4 Preheat the oven to 140°C/275°F/ Gas 1. Prepare 1 baking sheet, drawing a 23cm/9in circle in heavy pencil on the reverse of the paper.

5 Spread half the mixture into a thick, flat neat round, then spoon the rest in high swirls around the edge to create a border. Add to the border to give more height if you have any extra meringue mixture. Bake for 1–1½ hours until the meringue is firm, checking frequently to avoid the meringue overcooking and turning brown.

6 When cooked and cooled, peel off the paper and fill the pavlova shell with whipped cream and fresh fruit.

ICINGS, FROSTINGS AND FILLINGS

Toppings and fillings make a great final touch to an already delicious cake, making it even more appealing. Soft and creamy toppings and fillings, such as American frosting and crème pâtissière, can add extra moisture to a cake and enhance its flavour, while a more formal icing (frosting), such as royal icing, can make an impressive centrepiece at a wedding or special birthday.

Making Royal Icing

Royal icing is the traditional coating for formal celebration cakes, made from fruit cake, especially wedding cakes. Finely sifted icing (confectioners') sugar and egg white are blended to a soft or firm mixture depending on whether it is to be used for coating or piping.

Royal icing is easy to make using an electric beater. A little lemon juice is usually added and a little glycerine can also be mixed in to prevent the icing from setting too hard. As it is white, the icing can be coloured easily. The icing must be kept covered when not in use as a crust soon forms on its surface, producing lumps.

1 Whisk 1 egg white and lemon juice in a large mixing bowl until the egg white is slightly broken down, but not too frothy. Then sift in the icing sugar a little at a time, whisking well after each addition. Usually, 1 large egg white will take up 450g/1lb sugar, but add as much as required to give a light icing with a soft spreading texture. For piping, add slightly more icing sugar.

2 Keep whisking hard until the icing is smooth and stands in very stiff peaks. If you add too much sugar, add water drop by drop, whisking constantly.

Making Marzipan

This almond paste is applied to fruit cakes to give a smooth surface for the royal icing and to prevent any colour or oiliness from seeping through the icing. Marzipan is also used to make sweets and model novelties. It can be baked into cakes, such as Austrian Christmas stollen and British Easter simnel cake.

1 Sift 225g/8oz/2 cups icing (confectioners') sugar into a mixing bowl. Add 225g/8oz/2 cups ground almonds and a few drops of almond essence. Add 1 egg yolk and mix lightly, adding cold water if necessary, to form a firm dough that can be rolled.

2 Wrap tightly in clear film and chill until required. Use within 1 week.

Making American Frosting

While royal icing is formal and firm, American frosting is a light, soft coating, with a mallow-like texture and a crisp outer coating, which complements light cakes, such as a carrot cake, perfectly.

American frosting is made in less than 10 minutes, but is best whisked until cool before it is used. It keeps well for several days until the cake is cut but once the crisp outer layer is broken, it is best if consumed within a day.

1 In a large, clean bowl, mix 150g/5oz/ ¾ cup caster (superfine) sugar with 15ml/1 tbsp water, 15ml/1 tbsp golden (light corn) syrup and 1 large (US X large) egg white. Stand the bowl over a pan of simmering water and whisk gently until the sugar has dissolved.

2 Whisk hard for several minutes, until the mixture forms stiff peaks. Remove from the heat and continue whisking until the frosting is cool and thick enough to spread over or round a cake. Use promptly, then leave to cool.

Using albumen powder

This pasteurized product can be used to making a hard royal icing and is ideal if you are concerned about serving food containing raw eggs. Blend the powder with water to make a smooth paste, dilute according to the instructions on the packet, then make royal icing in the usual way.

Making Meringue Butter Icing

This rich and glossy icing is quite unlike the bland butter icing made from butter and sugar. It is ideal for spreading, coating and piping and gives a very crisp professional look. Meringue butter icing is made by whisking a sugar syrup into egg whites, then combining the mixture with softened butter. A richer version can be made using egg yolks instead of whites and produces a yellower icing.

1 Dissolve 115g/4oz/½ cup sugar in 90ml/6 tbsp water and then boil to the sugar syrup stage (115°C/239°F).

2 Put 4 egg whites in a large bowl and whisk in the sugar syrup, over a pan of gently simmering water. Continue whisking until the mixture is very thick and glossy.

3 Cream 225g/8oz/1 cup good quality unsalted butter in a bowl until soft.

4 Using an electric beater, gently work the butter into the meringue mixture until you have a firm glossy consistency.

5 Mix in a few drops of vanilla essence (extract) if you wish, then allow the icing to cool before spreading over the top and sides of the cake.

6 To make a richer butter cream, use egg yolks instead of whites. Lightly beat 4 egg yolks in a bowl, then slowly whisk in the syrup over a pan of simmering water. Keep whisking until it thickens, forming a mousse-like consistency and turning a pale cream colour. Remove from the heat and allow to cool a little, then gently work the creamed butter into the egg mixture.

7 To make a rich chocolate butter cream, work about 115g/4oz melted dark chocolate into the cooled icing until smooth.

Making Crème Pâtissière

Also known as confectioners' custard, this rich and creamy mixture is used to fill cakes, pastries, tarts and flans, or as the base for rich ice creams. Being thickened with flour, it is easy to make, keeps well and can be spread or piped. Whipped double (heavy) cream, butter cream or Italian meringue can be added to lighten the custard if you find it too rich. Flavoured crème pâtissière is also delicious, and is very easy to make. To flavour with coffee, simply dissolve 30ml/2 tbsp instant coffee in to the milk, or to flavour with chocolate, beat 150g/5oz melted bitter chocolate into the custard.

1 Beat 6 egg yolks with 45ml/3 tbsp plain (all-purpose) flour and 115g/4oz caster (sugar) sugar to make a paste.

2 Heat 550ml/18fl oz/2¼ cups milk with a little vanilla essence (extract) until boiling. Remove from the heat and strain into the paste, whisking well.

3 When thoroughly blended, pour the mixture back into the pan and cook gently, whisking constantly, until it begins to thicken. Then whisk continuously until the mixture boils, becomes thick, glossy and smooth.

4 Remove the pan from the heat and continue whisking until cooled slightly. Cover the surface of the mixture closely with clear film and leave until ready to use or set aside to cool. When cold, beat well to remove any lumps.

BASIC MICROWAVE METHODS

With a little know-how and, in some cases, a few special items of cooking equipment, eggs can be cooked very successfully in the microwave. Some traditional methods, however, have to be avoided; for example, boiled eggs. Whole eggs, which have not been broken or beaten, must be pierced before cooking to prevent steam from building up in their outer membrane and exploding. Microwave cooking can speed up most egg dishes, especially time-consuming sauces and custards.

Microwave Steam-boiling

Traditional boiling is out of the question when using a microwave. However, a similar final result can be achieved using a four-egg container that holds water underneath the eggs and produces a steam-boiled egg. Pierce the shell, close the lid and cook according to the manufacturer's instructions.

Poaching Eggs in the Microwave

To poach an egg in the microwave, pour 60ml/4 tbsp water and 1.5ml/¼ tsp vinegar into a ramekin dish or custard cup and heat on full power for 1 minute or until boiling. Carefully break the egg into the water, pierce the yolk twice, cover with oiled greaseproof or waxed paper and cook on full power for

30 seconds. Leave the egg in the water for about 2 minutes, or longer for firmer eggs, before draining well and serving.

Alternatively, a special microwave egg poacher can be used following the manufacturer's instructions.

Frying in a Browning Dish

A browning dish can be used for frying eggs. Preheat the dish on full power for 2–3 minutes, or according to the manufacturer's instructions. Add a little butter and tilt the dish to coat it well, then break in the egg. Gently pierce the yolk, season the egg to taste, cover and cook for 30–60 seconds on full power, depending on the size of the egg.

Scrambling Eggs in the Microwave

Melt 7.5ml/½ tbsp butter for each egg in a bowl on full power for 30 seconds. In another bowl, beat the eggs with seasoning and 15ml/1 tbsp milk for each egg. Add the eggs to the butter and beat well. Cook on full power, allowing about 45 seconds for each egg, stirring every 30 seconds. Cook until the eggs are very softly scrambled, then leave them to stand for 1–2 minutes. The eggs will continue to set while standing.

Making a Microwave Omelette

Omelettes are easy to make using a specially designed two-sided microwave omelette dish.

1 Heat 25g/1oz/2 tbsp butter in an omelette dish on full power for 1 minute. Beat 3 eggs with seasoning and divide them between the two sides of the dish.

2 Microwave on 50% power for 3–4 minutes. Use a spatula to stir the egg, pulling in the cooked sides, and then cook for a further 3 minutes. Allow to stand for 1 minute before serving.

Microwave Meringues

Traditional meringues with a gooey centre cannot be made in a microwave. Microwave meringues are dry and crisp, but are still delicious.

1 Beat 1 egg white with 275g/10oz/ 1½ cups icing (confectioners') sugar until the mixture forms a stiff ball. You may need a little more sugar.

2 Roll the mixture into about 25 balls, the size of a walnut, and place about 5 balls well apart on microwave baking paper or in paper cake cups. Cook on full power for 1–1½ minutes, until the mixture puffs up to about four times its original size. Leave to cool. Repeat with the remaining batches of mixture.

MAKING SAUCES IN THE MICROWAVE

Egg and butter sauces can be difficult to prepare by the traditional method, but are simple to make in the microwave. They can also be reheated in the microwave after conventional cooking. Cover the cooled sauce with buttered greaseproof (waxed) paper or clear film and reheat on full power in bursts of 30 seconds, beating frequently.

Making Hollandaise Sauce

1 Beat 2 egg yolks in a bowl with 30ml/ 2 tbsp white wine vinegar or lemon juice and seasoning. Heat 115g/4oz/ ½ cup butter in a bowl on full power for about 1½ minutes or until bubbling. Pour the butter slowly into the egg yolks, whisking constantly.

2 Cook on full power in bursts of 15 seconds, whisking after each burst, until the sauce coats the back of a spoon. Leave to stand for 2 minutes, whisking, as the sauce thickens.

Making Béarnaise Sauce

Place 60ml/4 tbsp tarragon vinegar, 1 chopped shallot, a pinch of cayenne pepper and 15ml/1 tbsp chopped fresh parsley and tarragon in a microwaveable bowl. Heat on full power for 3 minutes, or until reduced by about half. Continue as for hollandaise sauce.

MAKING CUSTARDS IN THE MICROWAVE

Classic custards are quickly and easily made in the microwave. Add cornflour (cornstarch) to prevent curdling.

Making Custard Sauce

To make a pouring custard, heat 300ml/ ½ pint/1¼ cups milk with a few drops of vanilla essence (extract), for 2 minutes, until almost boiling. Whisk 2 eggs with 30ml/2 tbsp sugar and 15ml/1 tbsp cornflour (cornstarch), then whisk in the hot milk. Cook on full power for bursts of about 30 seconds, whisking each time, until thickened. Leave to stand for 1 minute and whisk before serving.

Making Set Custard

For set custard, heat 600ml/1 pint/ 2½ cups milk in a large bowl on full power for 3 minutes. Whisk 4 eggs with 25g/1oz caster (superfine) sugar, then whisk in a little of the hot milk. Pour the eggs back into the milk, whisking well. Strain the mixture into 4 ramekins with fruit in the base. Cook on defrost for about 14 minutes or until the custards are set. Cool, then chill before serving.

Making Crème Caramel

Put 50g/2oz/4 tbsp caster (superfine) sugar and 30ml/2 tbsp water into a microwaveable dish and cook, uncovered, on full power for 2 minutes, until the mixture turns a pale straw colour. Stir in 90ml/6 tbsp water and microwave for 2 minutes until golden. Wearing oven gloves, swirl the caramel around the bowl, then leave to cool. Prepare the custard, using half milk and half double (heavy) cream, pour into the coated dish and cook as for set custard.

COOKING
WITH
EGGS

*Eggs are both delicious and versatile, and can
be used in a huge range of dishes. They are
wonderful served on their own — poached,
boiled, fried or scrambled — but they can also
create exciting and unusual dishes when
combined with other ingredients. Light and
fluffy soufflés, crisp meringues, succulent cakes
and moist omelettes are just a few of the
mouthwatering dishes that can
be made with eggs.*

BREAKFASTS AND BRUNCHES

Eggs first became an important breakfast food in the Victorian era.

Nowadays, eggs have become a key ingredient, both for breakfasts and lazy

weekend brunches, and are used to create enticing dishes that are a far cry

from plain boiled eggs or poached eggs on toast.

Eggs make a perfect start to the day, providing plenty of energy to keep you

going. This chapter includes classic breakfast and brunch dishes, such as

Eggs Benedict, Scrambled Eggs with Smoked Salmon, and Kedgeree,

as well as more unusual recipes, such as Shirred Eggs

with Pancetta, and Tomato and

Courgette Timbales.

EGGS BENEDICT

THERE IS STILL DEBATE OVER WHO CREATED THIS RECIPE BUT THE MOST LIKELY STORY CREDITS MR AND MRS LEGRAND BENEDICT, REGULARS AT NEW YORK'S DELMONICO'S RESTAURANT, WHO COMPLAINED THERE WAS NOTHING NEW ON THE MENU. THIS DISH WAS CREATED AS A RESULT.

SERVES FOUR

INGREDIENTS
  4 eggs
  2 English muffins or 4 slices
    of bread
  butter, for spreading
  4 thick slices cooked ham, cut
    to fit the muffins
  fresh chives, to garnish
For the sauce
  3 egg yolks
  30ml/2 tbsp fresh lemon juice
  1.5ml/¼ tsp salt
  115g/4oz/½ cup butter
  30ml/2 tbsp single (light) cream
  ground black pepper

COOK'S TIP
Use only very fresh eggs for poaching, because they keep their shape better in the water.

1 To make the sauce, blend the egg yolks, lemon juice and salt in a food processor or blender for 15 seconds.

2 Melt the butter in a small pan until it bubbles, but do not let it brown. With the motor running, slowly drizzle the melted butter into the food processor or blender through the feed tube in a slow, steady stream. Turn off the machine as soon as all the butter has been added.

3 Pour the sauce into a bowl, placed over a pan of simmering water. Stir for 2–3 minutes, until thickened. If the sauce begins to curdle, whisk in 15ml/1 tbsp boiling water. Stir in the cream and season with pepper. Remove from the heat and keep warm over the pan.

4 Bring a shallow pan of lightly salted water to the boil. Break each egg into a cup, then slide it carefully into the water. Delicately turn the white around the yolk with a spoon. Cook for about 4 minutes until the white is set. Remove the eggs from the pan, one at a time, using a slotted spoon, and drain on kitchen paper. Cut off any ragged edges with a small knife or scissors.

5 While the eggs are poaching, split and toast the muffins or toast the slices of bread. Spread with butter while still warm.

6 Place a piece of ham, which you may brown in butter if you wish, on each muffin half or slice of toast, then place an egg on each ham-topped muffin. Spoon the warm sauce over the eggs, garnish with chives and serve.

SOUFFLÉ OMELETTE WITH MUSHROOMS

A SOUFFLÉ OMELETTE MAKES AN IDEAL MEAL FOR ONE, ESPECIALLY WITH THIS DELICIOUS FILLING.
USE A COMBINATION OF DIFFERENT MUSHROOMS, SUCH AS OYSTER OR CHESTNUT, IF YOU LIKE.

SERVES ONE

INGREDIENTS
  2 eggs, separated
  15g/½oz/1 tbsp butter
  flat leaf parsley or coriander
    (cilantro) leaves, to garnish
For the mushroom sauce
  15g/½oz/1 tbsp butter
  75g/3oz/generous 1 cup button
    (white) mushrooms, thinly sliced
  15ml/1 tbsp plain (all-purpose) flour
  85–120ml/3–4fl oz/⅓–½ cup milk
  5ml/1 tsp chopped fresh
    parsley (optional)
  salt and ground black pepper

1 To make the mushroom sauce, melt the butter in a pan or frying pan and add the sliced mushrooms. Fry gently for 4–5 minutes, stirring occasionally, until tender.

2 Stir in the flour, then gradually add the milk, stirring all the time. Cook until boiling and thickened. Add the parsley, if using, and season with salt and pepper. Keep warm.

3 Beat the egg yolks with 15ml/1 tbsp water and season with a little salt and pepper. Whisk the egg whites until stiff, then fold into the egg yolks using a metal spoon. Preheat the grill (broiler).

4 Melt the butter in a large frying pan and pour the egg mixture into the pan. Cook over a gentle heat for 2–4 minutes. Place the frying pan under the grill and cook for a further 3–4 minutes until the top is golden brown.

5 Slide the omelette on to a warmed serving plate, pour the mushroom sauce over the top and fold the omelette in half. Serve, garnished with parsley or coriander leaves.

COOK'S TIP
For extra flavour, add a few drops of Worcestershire sauce to the mushrooms as they cook.

SCRAMBLED EGGS WITH SMOKED SALMON

FOR A LUXURY BREAKFAST, OR A LATE-NIGHT SUPPER, YOU CAN'T BEAT THIS VERY SPECIAL COMBINATION. TRY IT ON CHRISTMAS MORNING ALONG WITH A GLASS OF CHAMPAGNE MIXED WITH FRESHLY SQUEEZED ORANGE JUICE.

SERVES FOUR

INGREDIENTS
    4 slices of wholemeal (whole-wheat)
      bread, crusts trimmed
    50g/2oz/4 tbsp butter
    115g/4oz thinly sliced
      smoked salmon
    6 eggs
    45–60ml/3–4 tbsp double
      (heavy) cream
    60ml/4 tbsp crème fraîche
    salt and ground black pepper
    generous 60ml/4 tbsp lumpfish roe
      or salmon caviar and sprigs of dill,
      to garnish

COOK'S TIP
If you are lucky enough to have a fresh
truffle, grate a little into the scrambled
eggs. Serve them on toast, topped with
a little chopped fresh chervil.

1 Spread the slices of bread with half of
the butter and arrange the smoked
salmon on top. Cut each slice in half
and set aside while you make the
scrambled eggs.

2 Lightly beat the eggs together and
season with salt and freshly ground
pepper. Melt the remaining butter in
a pan until sizzling, then quickly stir
in the beaten eggs.

3 Stir the eggs constantly until they
begin to thicken. Just before they have
finished cooking, stir in the double
cream. Remove the pan from the heat
and stir in the crème fraîche. Set the
eggs aside and keep warm.

4 Spoon the scrambled eggs on to the
smoked salmon. Top each serving with
a spoonful of caviar and serve,
garnished with sprigs of dill.

EGG CROSTINI WITH ROUILLE

CROSTINI ARE EXTREMELY QUICK TO MAKE SO ARE PERFECT FOR BREAKFAST OR BRUNCH. THE ROUILLE GIVES THEM A HINT OF MEDITERRANEAN FLAVOUR. TRADITIONALLY, ROUILLE IS SERVED WITH THICK FISH SOUP, BUT HERE IT PROVIDES THE PERFECT COMPLEMENT TO LIGHTLY FRIED EGGS.

SERVES FOUR

INGREDIENTS
    4 slices of ciabatta bread
    extra virgin olive oil
    45ml/3 tbsp home-made mayonnaise
    5ml/1 tsp harissa
    4 eggs
    4 small slices smoked ham
    watercress or other salad leaves,
      to serve

COOK'S TIP
Harissa is a fiery North African chilli paste
made from dried red chillies, cumin, garlic,
coriander, caraway and olive oil. It adds a
sweet spicy taste to dips, sauces and stews,
and makes a great addition to mayonnaise
for serving with meat or fish dishes.

1 Preheat the oven to 200°C/400°F/
Gas 6. Use a pastry brush to brush
each slice of ciabatta bread lightly with
a little olive oil. Place the bread on a
baking sheet and bake for 10 minutes
or until crisp and turning golden brown.

2 Meanwhile, make the rouille. Mix
together the mayonnaise and harissa.
Fry the eggs lightly in a very little oil in
a non-stick pan.

3 Top the baked bread with the ham,
eggs and a small spoonful of rouille.
Serve immediately with watercress.

SHIRRED EGGS WITH PANCETTA

*THESE EGGS ARE BAKED WITH ITALIAN BACON IN INDIVIDUAL OVENPROOF DISHES. YOU COULD ADD
OTHER INGREDIENTS, SUCH AS SPICY SAUSAGE OR SAUTÉED SPINACH.*

SERVES FOUR

INGREDIENTS
    50g/2oz/4 tbsp butter
    115g/4oz pancetta, sliced
    8 eggs
    bunch of rocket (arugula)
    squeeze of lemon juice
    15ml/1 tbsp olive oil
    ground black pepper

COOK'S TIP
For hungry guests, use very large double-
yolk eggs for this dish and serve with lots
of freshly baked ciabatta bread spread
with unsalted butter.

1 Preheat the oven to 200°C/400°F/
Gas 6. Divide half the butter and all of
the pancetta among 4 individual serving
or gratin dishes.

2 Bake for 8–10 minutes until the
pancetta is sizzling, then carefully
remove the dishes from the oven.

3 Crack 2 eggs into each dish, add
another knob (pat) of butter to each
and sprinkle with seasoning. Return to
the oven for a further 7–8 minutes or
until the eggs are just set.

4 Toss the rocket in the lemon juice and
oil, and add some to each dish.

TOMATO AND COURGETTE TIMBALES

*THESE BAKED SAVOURY CUSTARDS ARE TYPICAL OF SOUTHERN FRENCH COOKING. THE EGG AND
VEGETABLE COMBINATION IS DELICIOUS; SERVE WARM OR COOL AS A LIGHT MEAL, AN ACCOMPANIMENT
TO A MAIN MEAL, OR AN APPETIZER.*

SERVES FOUR

INGREDIENTS
    a little butter
    2 courgettes (zucchini)
    2 firm, ripe vine tomatoes, sliced
    2 eggs and 2 egg yolks
    45ml/3 tbsp double (heavy) cream
    15ml/1 tbsp fresh tomato sauce or
        passata (bottled strained tomatoes)
    10ml/2 tsp chopped fresh basil or
        oregano or 5ml/1 tsp dried
    salt and ground black pepper
    sautéed potatoes, to serve

VARIATIONS
Replace the courgettes with chopped
asparagus or aubergine (eggplant). Steam
the asparagus for 3–7 minutes and the
aubergine for 3–4 minutes.

1 Preheat the oven to 180°C/350°F/
Gas 4. Lightly butter 4 large ramekins or
individual ovenproof dishes.

2 Trim the courgettes, then cut them
into thin slices. Put them into a
steamer, place over a pan of boiling
water, cover with a lid and steam for
4–5 minutes. Shake the steamer to get
rid of as much moisture as possible,
then layer the courgettes in the
ramekins with the sliced tomatoes.

3 Whisk together the eggs, cream,
tomato sauce or passata, herbs and
seasoning. Pour the egg mixture into
the ramekins, dividing it evenly. Place in
a roasting pan and half fill the pan with
hot water. Bake for 20–30 minutes until
the custard is just firm.

4 Cool slightly then run a knife around
the rims. Carefully turn out on to small
plates. Serve with sautéed potatoes.

KEDGEREE

A POPULAR BREAKFAST DISH IN VICTORIAN ENGLAND, KEDGEREE HAS ITS ORIGINS IN KHICHRI, AN INDIAN RICE AND LENTIL DISH, AND IS OFTEN FLAVOURED OR TOPPED WITH CURRY POWDER.

SERVES FOUR

INGREDIENTS

500g/1¼lb smoked haddock
115g/4oz/generous ½ cup long
  grain rice
30ml/2 tbsp lemon juice
150ml/¼ pint/⅔ cup single (light)
  or sour cream
pinch of freshly grated nutmeg
pinch of cayenne pepper
2 eggs, hard-boiled (hard-cooked)
  and peeled, cut into wedges
50g/2oz/4 tbsp butter, cubed, plus
  extra for greasing
30ml/2 tbsp chopped fresh parsley
salt and ground black pepper

1 Poach the haddock, just covered by water, for about 10 minutes, until the flesh flakes easily. Lift the fish from the cooking liquid using a slotted spoon, then remove any skin and bones, and flake the fish.

2 Pour the rice into a measuring jug (cup) and note the volume, then tip out, pour the fish cooking liquid into the jug and top up with water, until it measures twice the volume of the rice.

3 Bring the fish cooking liquid to the boil, add the rice, stir, then cover and simmer for about 15 minutes, until the rice is tender and the liquid absorbed. Meanwhile, preheat the oven to 180°C/ 350°F/Gas 4, and butter a baking dish.

4 Remove the rice from the heat and stir in the lemon juice, cream, flaked fish, nutmeg and cayenne. Gently stir the egg wedges into the rice.

5 Tip the rice mixture into the baking dish, dot with butter, cover with kitchen foil and bake for about 25 minutes.

6 Stir the chopped parsley into the kedgeree, check the seasoning and serve at once.

COOK'S TIP
Taste the Kedgeree before you add salt, since the smoked haddock may already be quite salty.

AMERICAN PANCAKES WITH BACON

THESE SMALL, THICK, BUTTERY PANCAKES WILL BE EATEN IN SECONDS, SO MAKE PLENTY. THE BATTER CAN BE MADE THE NIGHT BEFORE, READY FOR BREAKFAST.

MAKES ABOUT TWENTY

INGREDIENTS

175g/6oz/1½ cups plain (all-purpose)
  flour, sifted
pinch of salt
15ml/1 tbsp caster (superfine) sugar
2 large (US X large) eggs
150ml/¼ pint/⅔ cup milk
5ml/1 tsp bicarbonate of soda
  (baking soda)
10ml/2 tsp cream of tartar
oil, for cooking
butter
maple syrup
crisply grilled (broiled) bacon,
  to serve

1 To make the batter, mix together the flour, salt and sugar. In a separate bowl, beat the eggs and milk together, then gradually stir into the flour, beating to a smooth, thick consistency. Add the bicarbonate of soda and cream of tartar, mix well, then cover and chill until ready to cook.

2 When you are ready to cook the pancakes, beat the batter again. Heat a little oil in a heavy frying pan or griddle. Drop dessertspoonfuls of the mixture into the pan, spaced well apart, and cook over a fairly high heat until bubbles appear on the surface of the pancakes and the undersides become golden brown.

3 Carefully turn the pancakes over with a palette knife or spatula and cook briefly until golden underneath, then transfer them to a heated serving dish. Top each pancake with a little butter and drizzle with maple syrup. Serve with grilled bacon.

SOUPS, APPETIZERS AND SNACKS

The versatility of eggs, combined with their decorative nature, make them the

ideal ingredient for a whole range of deliciously tempting soups, appetizers

and snacks. The delicate flavour of Egg and Avocado Mousses will whet

the appetite of any dinner party guest, while warming Saffron Fish Soup

is the perfect start to a sophisticated winter soirée.

For a light pre-dinner snack, try tiny Quail's Eggs with Herbs or

Crab Egg Rolls, or, for those with a heartier appetite,

Thai Fish Cakes with Egg or Tunisian Brik are delicious at

any time of the day or night.

SAFFRON FISH SOUP

FILLING YET NOT TOO RICH, THIS GOLDEN SOUP WILL MAKE A DELICIOUS MEAL ON EARLY SUMMER EVENINGS, SERVED WITH LOTS OF HOT FRESH BREAD AND A GLASS OF FRUITY, DRY WHITE WINE. WHEN MUSSELS ARE NOT AVAILABLE, USE PRAWNS OR SHRIMP IN THEIR SHELLS INSTEAD.

SERVES FOUR

INGREDIENTS

1 parsnip, quartered
2 carrots, quartered
1 onion, quartered
2 celery sticks, quartered
2 smoked bacon rashers (strips),
   rinds removed
juice of 1 lemon
pinch of saffron threads
450g/1lb fish heads
450g/1lb live mussels, scrubbed
1 leek, shredded
2 shallots, finely chopped
30ml/2 tbsp chopped dill, plus extra
   sprigs to garnish
450g/1lb haddock, skinned and boned
3 egg yolks
30ml/2 tbsp double (heavy) cream
salt and ground black pepper

1 Put the parsnip, carrots, onion, celery, bacon, lemon juice, saffron threads and fish heads in a large pan with 900ml/1½ pints/3¾ cups water and bring to the boil. Boil gently for 20 minutes or until reduced by half.

COOK'S TIP
Fish stock freezes well and will keep for up to 6 months.

2 Discard any mussels that are open and don't close when tapped sharply. Add the rest to the pan of stock. Cook for about 4 minutes until they have opened. Strain the soup and return the liquid to the pan. Discard any unopened mussels, then remove the remaining ones from their shells and set aside.

3 Add the leeks and shallots to the soup, bring to the boil and cook for 5 minutes. Add the dill and haddock, and simmer for a further 5 minutes until the fish is tender. Remove the haddock, using a slotted spoon, then flake it into a bowl, using a fork.

4 In another bowl, whisk together the eggs and double cream. Whisk in a little of the hot soup, then whisk the mixture back into the hot but not boiling liquid. Continue to whisk for several minutes as it heats through and thickens slightly, but do not let it boil.

5 Add the flaked haddock and mussels to the soup and check the seasoning. Garnish with tiny sprigs of dill and serve piping hot.

EGG FLOWER SOUP

THIS SIMPLE, HEALTHY SOUP IS FLAVOURED WITH FRESH ROOT GINGER AND CHINESE FIVE-SPICE POWDER. IT IS QUICK AND DELICIOUS AND CAN BE MADE AT THE LAST MINUTE.

SERVES FOUR

INGREDIENTS

    1.2 litres/2 pints/5 cups fresh
      chicken or vegetable stock
    10ml/2 tsp peeled, grated fresh
      root ginger
    10ml/2 tsp light soy sauce
    5ml/1 tsp sesame oil
    5ml/1 tsp Chinese five-spice powder
    15–30ml/1–2 tbsp cornflour
      (cornstarch)
    2 eggs
    salt and ground black pepper
    1 spring onion (scallion), very finely
      sliced diagonally and 15ml/1 tbsp
      roughly chopped coriander (cilantro)
      or flat leaf parsley, to garnish

COOK'S TIP

This soup is a good way of using up
leftover egg yolks or whites.

1 Put the chicken or vegetable stock into a large pan with the ginger, soy sauce, oil and five-spice powder. Bring to the boil and allow to simmer gently for about 10 minutes.

2 Blend the cornflour in a measuring jug (cup) with 60–75ml/4–5 tbsp water and stir into the stock. Cook, stirring constantly, until slightly thickened. Season to taste.

3 In a jug, beat the eggs together with 30ml/2 tbsp cold water until the mixture becomes frothy.

4 Bring the soup back just to the boil and drizzle in the egg mixture, stirring vigorously with chopsticks. Choose a jug with a fine spout to form a very thin drizzle. Serve at once, sprinkled with the sliced spring onions and chopped coriander or parsley.

PARTY EGGS

EGGS MAKE PERFECT PARTY FOOD. GIVE THEM A VARIETY OF FILLINGS AND GARNISHES FOR A STUNNING CENTREPIECE.

EACH VARIATION FILLS SIX EGGS

EGGS WITH CAVIAR

INGREDIENTS

4 spring onions (scallions), trimmed
and very finely sliced
30ml/2 tbsp sour cream
5ml/1 tsp lemon juice
25g/1oz/2 tbsp caviar
salt and ground black pepper
lemon rind and caviar, to garnish

1 Mix all the ingredients with the egg yolks, spoon back into the egg whites and garnish with lemon rind and caviar.

NUTTY DEVILLED EGGS

INGREDIENTS

40g/1½oz cooked ham, chopped
4 walnut halves, very finely chopped
15ml/1 tbsp Dijon mustard
15ml/1 tbsp mayonnaise
5ml/1 tsp white wine vinegar
few large pinches of cayenne pepper
salt and ground black pepper
paprika and gherkins, to garnish

1 Mix together all the ingredients with the egg yolks, spoon into the whites and garnish with paprika and gherkin slices.

PRAWN AND CUCUMBER EGGS

INGREDIENTS

75g/3oz/½ cup cooked peeled prawns
(shrimp), reserving 12 for garnish
and the rest chopped
25g/1oz cucumber, peeled
and diced
5ml/1 tsp tomato sauce
15ml/1 tbsp lemon mayonnaise
salt and ground black pepper
fennel sprigs, to garnish

1 Mix all the ingredients with the egg yolks, spoon back into the egg whites and garnish with prawns and fennel.

GARLIC AND GREEN PEPPERCORN EGGS

INGREDIENTS

5ml/1 tsp garlic purée (paste) or
1 large garlic clove, crushed
45ml/3 tbsp whipped cream
or crème fraîche
salt and ground black pepper
2.5ml/½ tsp green peppercorns,
crushed, to garnish

1 Mix the garlic, cream, egg yolks and seasoning. Place in a piping bag and pipe into the egg whites. Sprinkle with a few crushed peppercorns.

BAKED EGGS WITH CREAMY LEEKS

THIS SIMPLE BUT ELEGANT APPETIZER CAN ALSO BE MADE WITH OTHER VEGETABLES SUCH AS PURÉED SPINACH OR RATATOUILLE. IT IS PERFECT FOR LAST-MINUTE ENTERTAINING OR QUICK DINING.

SERVES FOUR

INGREDIENTS
15g/½oz/1 tbsp butter, plus extra
   for greasing
225g/8oz small leeks, thinly sliced
75–90ml/5–6 tbsp whipping cream
freshly grated nutmeg
4 small–medium (US medium–
   large) eggs
a few sage leaves
sunflower oil
salt and ground black pepper

VARIATION
For a slightly different result, beat the eggs with the remaining cream and seasoning in step 4 and spoon over the leeks. Bake as normal.

1 Preheat the oven to 190°C/375°F/ Gas 5. Generously butter the base and sides of 4 ramekins.

2 Melt the butter in a frying pan and cook the leeks for 3–5 minutes over a medium heat, stirring frequently, until softened but not browned.

3 Add 45ml/3 tbsp of the cream and cook over a gentle heat for 5 minutes until the leeks are very soft and the cream has thickened a little. Season with salt, pepper and nutmeg.

4 Place the ramekins in a small roasting pan and divide the leeks among them. Break an egg into each, spoon over the remaining cream, and season.

5 Pour boiling water into the pan to come about halfway up the sides of the dishes. Transfer to the oven and bake for about 10 minutes, until just set.

6 While the eggs are baking, fry the sage leaves in a little oil until crisp and scatter over the top of the eggs to serve.

EGG <u>AND</u> AVOCADO MOUSSES

LIGHT AND CREAMY, WITH LOTS OF TEXTURE AND A DELICIOUS COMBINATION OF FLAVOURS, THESE LITTLE MOUSSES ARE BEST SERVED ON THE DAY YOU MAKE THEM, BUT CHILL REALLY WELL FIRST.

SERVES SIX

INGREDIENTS

olive oil, for greasing
11g/¼oz sachet gelatine
juice and rind of 1 lemon
60ml/4 tbsp good mayonnaise
60ml/4 tbsp chopped fresh dill
5ml/1 tsp anchovy essence (paste)
5ml/1 tsp Worcestershire sauce
4 eggs, hard-boiled (hard-cooked),
  peeled and chopped
175g/6oz/1 cup cooked, peeled
  prawns (shrimp), roughly chopped
1 large ripe but just firm avocado,
  peeled, stoned (pitted) and diced
250ml/8fl oz/1 cup double (heavy) or
  whipping cream, lightly whipped
2 egg whites
salt and ground black pepper
sprigs of dill, to garnish
Granary (whole-wheat) toast, to serve

1 Lightly grease 6 small ramekins, then wrap a piece of greaseproof (waxed) paper tightly around each of the dishes to form a collar. Ensure the paper comes well above the top of the dish, allowing plenty of room for the mousse to stand above the top of the dish. Secure firmly with tape so that the paper will support the mousse as it sets. If you prefer, prepare 1 small soufflé dish rather than individual ramekins.

2 Place the gelatine, lemon juice and 15ml/1 tbsp hot water in a small bowl, and place over a pan of hot water. Stir until the mixture becomes clear. Cool slightly, then blend in the lemon rind, mayonnaise, dill and sauces.

3 Mix the chopped hard-boiled eggs, prawns and avocado in a medium bowl. Stir in the gelatine mixture, then fold in the whipped cream. Whisk the egg whites until holding soft peaks and fold into the mixture with seasoning to taste. Spoon into the ramekins and chill for about 4 hours. Garnish with dill and serve with toast.

COOK'S TIP

Other fish or shellfish can make a good alternative to prawns. Try substituting the same quantity of smoked trout or cooked crab meat.

QUAIL'S EGGS WITH HERBS

FOR AL FRESCO EATING OR LIGHT ENTERTAINING, THIS PLATTER OF CONTRASTING TASTES AND
TEXTURES IS PERFECT FOR A RELAXED ATMOSPHERE. THE PRETTY SHELLS OF THE QUAIL'S EGGS
ADD EXTRA APPEAL TO THIS DELIGHTFUL APPETIZER.

SERVES SIX

INGREDIENTS
    1 large Italian focaccia or 2–3 Indian
      parathas or other flatbreads
    olive oil, for brushing and dipping
    1 large garlic clove, finely chopped
    small handful of fresh mixed herbs,
      such as coriander (cilantro), mint,
      parsley and oregano, chopped
    18–24 quail's eggs
    30ml/2 tbsp home-made mayonnaise
    30ml/2 tbsp sour cream
    5ml/1 tsp chopped capers
    5ml/1 tsp finely chopped shallot
    225g/8oz fresh beetroot (beets),
      cooked in water, peeled and sliced
    ½ bunch spring onions (scallions),
      trimmed and halved lengthways
    60ml/4 tbsp red onion or tamarind
      and date chutney
    coarse sea salt
    mixed peppercorns, roughly ground

1 Preheat the oven to 190°C/375°F/
Gas 5. Brush the bread with olive oil,
sprinkle with garlic, mixed herbs and
seasoning, and bake for 10–15 minutes,
or until golden. Keep warm.

2 Put the quail's eggs into a pan of cold
water. Bring the water to the boil and
cook for 5 minutes. Lift the eggs out
of the pan, using a slotted spoon, and
place them in a bowl of cold water.
Leave to cool.

3 Make the mayonnaise dip. Mix
together the mayonnaise, sour cream,
capers, shallot and seasoning. Peel the
eggs or leave the guests to shell their
own, and arrange in a serving dish.

4 Cut the bread into wedges and serve
with the eggs and mayonnaise dip,
along with dishes of beetroot, onions
and chutney. Serve with bowls of coarse
salt, ground peppercorns and olive oil
for dipping.

THAI FISH CAKES ~~WITH~~ EGG

THESE TANGY LITTLE FISH CAKES, WITH A KICK OF EASTERN SPICE CAN BE SERVED AS A LIGHT SNACK OR PARTY FOOD BUT ALSO MAKE A GREAT BREAKFAST OR BRUNCH.

MAKES ABOUT TWENTY

INGREDIENTS

225g/8oz undyed smoked cod
  or haddock
225g/8oz fresh cod or haddock
1 small fresh red chilli, seeded
  and finely chopped
2 garlic cloves, chopped
1 lemon grass stalk, finely chopped
2 large spring onions (scallions), very
  finely chopped
30ml/2 tbsp Thai fish sauce
  (nam pla) or 30ml/2 tbsp soy
  sauce and a few drops of anchovy
  essence (paste)
60ml/4 tbsp thick coconut milk
2 large (US X large) eggs, beaten
15ml/1 tbsp chopped fresh
  coriander (cilantro)
15ml/1 tbsp cornflour (cornstarch),
  plus more for moulding
oil, for frying
soy sauce, rice vinegar and/or Thai
  fish sauce, for dipping

1 Remove the skin and any bones from the fish. Set the white fish aside and place the smoked fish in a bowl of cold water. Leave to soak for 10 minutes. Dry well on kitchen paper. Chop the smoked and fresh fish roughly and place in a food processor.

COOK'S TIP
If you know that you will need these fish cakes in a hurry, fry them the day before you intend to serve them but do not allow them to colour. Like chips (French fries), you can quickly fry them until crisp and golden just before serving.

2 Add the chilli, garlic, lemon grass, onions, sauce and coconut milk, and process until the fish is well blended with the spices. Add the eggs and coriander, and blend for a further few seconds. Cover and chill for 1 hour.

3 To make the fish cakes, flour your hands with cornflour and shape large teaspoonfuls of fish mixture into neat balls, lightly coating each with flour.

4 Heat 5–7.5cm/2–3in oil in a medium pan until it is hot enough to turn a crust of bread golden in about 1 minute. Fry the fish balls, 5–6 at a time, turning them carefully with a slotted spoon for 2–3 minutes, until they turn golden all over. Remove with a slotted spoon and drain on kitchen paper. Keep the fish cakes warm in the oven until they are all cooked. Serve immediately with one or more of the dipping sauces.

CRAB EGG ROLLS

THESE WONDERFUL CRAB ROLLS ARE VERY SIMILAR TO AUTHENTIC CHINESE SPRING ROLLS. THEY ARE MADE WITH WAFER-THIN PANCAKES, WHICH PROVIDE THE VERY CRISP CASE FOR THE FILLING.

MAKES ABOUT TWELVE

INGREDIENTS
3 eggs
450ml/¾ pint/scant 2 cups water
175g/6oz/1½ cups plain
  (all-purpose) flour
2.5ml/½ tsp salt
oil, for deep-frying
lime wedges, to serve
45ml/3 tbsp light soy sauce mixed
  with 5ml/1 tsp sesame oil,
  for dipping
For the filling
225g/8oz/1⅓ cups white crab meat
3 spring onions (scallions), shredded
2.5cm/1in piece fresh root
  ginger, grated
2 large garlic cloves, chopped
115g/4oz beansprouts
15ml/1 tbsp soy sauce
10–15ml/2–3 tsp cornflour
  (cornstarch) blended with
  15ml/1 tbsp water
1 egg, separated
salt and ground black pepper

1 Make the egg wrappers. Lightly beat the eggs and gradually stir in the water. Sift the flour and salt into another bowl and work in the egg mixture. Blend to a smooth batter, then remove any lumps if necessary. Leave to rest for 20 minutes.

2 When ready to use, whisk the mixture and stir in 15ml/1 tbsp cold water.

COOK'S TIP
To make 18–20 smaller rolls, prepare smaller egg wrappers using an omelette pan 12.5–15cm/5–6in in diameter.

3 Lightly grease a 25cm/10in non-stick frying pan and heat gently. To make smooth, pale wrappers, the frying pan must be hot enough to set the batter, but should not be hot enough for the batter to brown, bubble or develop holes. Pour in about 45ml/3 tbsp batter and swirl round the pan to spread evenly and very thinly. Cook for 2 minutes or until loose underneath. There is no need to cook the pancake on the other side.

4 Stack the pancakes, cooked side upwards, between sheets of greaseproof (waxed) paper. Set aside.

5 Combine the crab meat, shredded spring onions, ginger, garlic, bean sprouts, soy sauce, cornflour, egg yolk and seasoning.

6 Lightly beat the egg white. Place a spoonful of filling in the middle of each pancake, brush the edges with egg white and fold into neat parcels, tucking in the ends in well.

7 Using a stacking bamboo steamer, arrange 4 parcels in each layer, cover with a lid and steam for 30 minutes. Alternatively, heat the oil in a deep-frying pan and when a small piece of bread turns light golden in 1 minute carefully add 4 of the parcels, fold side downwards. Cook for 1–2 minutes until golden and crisp. Remove with a slotted spoon and place on kitchen paper. Keep warm in the oven while you cook the remaining egg rolls.

8 Serve with the thoroughly combined dipping sauce and wedges of lime.

TUNISIAN BRIK

YOU CAN MAKE THESE LITTLE PARCELS INTO ANY SHAPE YOU LIKE, BUT THE MOST IMPORTANT THING IS TO SAFELY ENCASE THE EGG WHITE BEFORE IT STARTS TO RUN OUT.

SERVES SIX

INGREDIENTS
45ml/3 tbsp butter, melted
1 small red onion, finely chopped
150g/5oz chicken or turkey
  fillet, minced (ground)
1 large garlic clove, crushed
juice of ½ lemon
30ml/2 tbsp chopped fresh parsley
12 sheets of filo pastry, each about
  15cm × 25cm/6in × 10in
6 small (US medium) eggs, such as
  bantam, pheasant or guinea fowl
oil, for deep-frying
salt and ground black pepper

3 Carefully crack an egg into the hollow and be ready to fold up the pastry immediately so the egg white does not run out. Lift the right hand edge and fold it over to the left edge to enclose the filling and seal quickly, then fold the bottom left corner straight up and then fold the bottom left corner up to the right edge, forming a triangle.

4 Use the remaining pastry sheets and filling to make another 5 parcels, then heat the oil in a wok or heavy pan until a cube of bread turns golden in about 1½ minutes. Carefully add the pastries to the oil, 2–3 at a time, and cook until golden brown. Lift them out of the pan with a slotted spoon and drain on kitchen paper. Serve hot or cold.

1 Heat half the butter in a pan and gently sauté the onion for about 3 minutes until softened. Add the mince, garlic, lemon juice, parsley and seasoning, and cook, stirring with chopsticks, for 2–3 minutes until the meat is just cooked. Set aside to cool.

2 Place one sheet of pastry lengthways on the work surface and brush with melted butter; top with a second sheet. Brush the edges with butter and place one-sixth of the mixture to the bottom left side of the pastry sheet, about 2.5cm/1in from the bottom. Flatten the filling, making a slight hollow in it.

COOK'S TIP
If you prefer to cook these pastries in the oven, preheat it to 220°C/425°F/Gas 7. Brush the pastries with butter or beaten egg and cook for 8–10 minutes until golden and crisp.

LIGHT LUNCHES

Eggs are the perfect ingredient for a whole host of nutritious and tasty light meals. They are the ideal addition to salads, transforming them from a side dish into a meal in themselves. The classic Salad Niçoise makes an unbeatable summer lunch with its combination of crisp leaves, fresh tuna and boiled eggs, while Pasta Salad with Ham, Egg and Asparagus is delicious all year round.

Eggs also make a wonderful base to any number of light meals. Try a slice or two of Spicy Sausage and Cheese Tortilla or Quiche Lorraine served with a refreshing tomato salad or, alternatively, enjoy the melt-in-the-mouth sensation of a light and airy Classic Cheese Soufflé.

CAESAR SALAD

THIS MUCH-ENJOYED SALAD WAS CREATED BY CAESAR CORDONI IN TIJUANA IN 1924. BE SURE TO ADD THE SOFT EGGS AND GARLIC CROÛTONS AT THE LAST MINUTE.

3 Add the remaining olive oil to the salad leaves and season with salt and pepper. Toss to coat well.

4 Break the boiled eggs on top. Sprinkle with the lemon juice and toss well to combine the ingredients.

5 Add the grated Parmesan cheese and anchovies, if using, then toss again.

6 Sprinkle the croûtons on top of the salad and serve immediately.

COOK'S TIPS
To make a tangier dressing, mix the olive oil with 30ml/2 tbsp white wine vinegar, 2.5ml/½ tsp mustard, 5ml/1 tsp sugar, and salt and pepper.

SERVES SIX

INGREDIENTS
175ml/6fl oz/¾ cup salad oil, preferably olive oil
115g/4oz/2 cups French or Italian bread, cut in 2.5cm/ 1in cubes
1 large garlic clove, crushed with the flat side of a knife
1 cos (romaine) lettuce
2 eggs, boiled for 1 minute
120ml/4fl oz/½ cup lemon juice
50g/2oz/⅔ cup freshly grated Parmesan cheese
6 anchovy fillets, drained and finely chopped (optional)
salt and ground black pepper

1 Heat 50ml/2fl oz/¼ cup of the oil in a frying pan. Add the bread and garlic and fry, stirring and turning constantly, until the cubes are golden brown. Drain on kitchen paper and discard the garlic.

2 Tear large lettuce leaves into smaller pieces. Put all the lettuce in a bowl.

SALAD NIÇOISE

MADE WITH THE FRESHEST OF INGREDIENTS, THIS CLASSIC PROVENÇAL SALAD MAKES A SIMPLE YET UNBEATABLE SUMMER DISH. SERVE WITH COUNTRY-STYLE BREAD AND CHILLED WHITE WINE.

SERVES FOUR

INGREDIENTS

  115g/4oz green beans, trimmed and
    cut in half
  115g/4oz mixed salad leaves
  ½ small cucumber, thinly sliced
  4 ripe tomatoes, quartered
  50g/2oz can anchovies, drained and
    halved lengthways
  4 eggs, hard-boiled (hard-cooked)
  1 tuna steak, about 175g/6oz
  olive oil, for brushing
  ½ bunch small radishes, trimmed
  50g/2oz/½ cup small black olives
  salt and ground black pepper
For the dressing
  90ml/6 tbsp extra virgin olive oil
  2 garlic cloves, crushed
  15ml/1 tbsp white wine vinegar

4 Preheat the grill (broiler). Brush the tuna with oil and sprinkle with salt and pepper. Grill (broil) for 3–4 minutes on each side until cooked through. Allow to cool, then flake with a fork.

5 Arrange the flaked tuna, anchovies, quartered eggs, radishes and olives over the salad. Pour over the dressing and toss together lightly to combine. Serve at once.

1 To make the dressing, whisk together the oil, garlic and vinegar and season to taste with salt and pepper. Set aside.

2 Cook the green beans in a pan of boiling water for 2 minutes until just tender, then drain.

3 Mix together the salad leaves, sliced cucumber, tomatoes and green beans in a large, shallow bowl. Halve the anchovies lengthways and shell and quarter the eggs.

VARIATION
Opinions vary on whether Salad Niçoise should include potatoes but, if you like, include a few small cooked new potatoes.

PASTA SALAD WITH HAM, EGG AND ASPARAGUS

WHEN YOU THINK IT'S TOO HOT FOR PASTA, TRY SERVING IT IN A WARM SALAD. HERE IT IS COMBINED WITH HAM, EGGS AND ASPARAGUS. A MUSTARD DRESSING MADE FROM THE ASPARAGUS STEMS CREATES A RICH AND TANGY ACCOMPANIMENT.

SERVES FOUR

INGREDIENTS
  450g/1lb asparagus
  450g/1lb dried tagliatelle
  225g/8oz cooked ham, in 5mm/¼in
    thick slices, cut into fingers
  2 eggs, hard-boiled (hard-cooked)
    and sliced
  50g/2oz Parmesan cheese, shaved
  salt and ground black pepper
For the dressing
  50g/2oz cooked potato
  75ml/5 tbsp olive oil, preferably Sicilian
  15ml/1 tbsp lemon juice
  10ml/2 tsp Dijon mustard
  120ml/4fl oz/½ cup vegetable stock

COOK'S TIPS
Use sliced chicken instead of the ham or thin slices of softer Italian cheese, such as Fontina or Asiago.

1 Trim and discard the tough woody part of the asparagus. Cut the spears in half and cook the thicker halves in boiling salted water for 12 minutes. After 6 minutes add the tips. Drain, then refresh under cold water until warm.

2 Finely chop 150g/5oz of the thick asparagus pieces. Place in a food processor with the dressing ingredients and process until smooth.

3 Boil the pasta in a large pan of salted water according to the packet instructions until tender. Refresh under cold water until warm, and drain.

4 To serve, toss the pasta with the asparagus sauce and divide among 4 pasta plates. Top with the ham, hard-boiled eggs and asparagus tips. Serve with a sprinkling of Parmesan cheese shavings.

SPECIAL FRIED RICE

MORE COLOURFUL AND ELABORATE THAN OTHER FRIED RICE DISHES, SPECIAL FRIED RICE IS ALMOST A MEAL IN ITSELF AND IS IDEAL FOR A MIDWEEK SUPPER.

SERVES FOUR

INGREDIENTS

50g/2oz/⅓ cup cooked peeled
   prawns (shrimp)
3 eggs
5ml/1 tsp salt
2 spring onions (scallions),
   finely chopped
60ml/4 tbsp vegetable oil
115g/4oz lean pork, finely diced
15ml/1 tbsp light soy sauce
15ml/1 tbsp Chinese rice wine
   or dry sherry
450g/1lb/6 cups cooked rice
115g/4oz green peas

COOK'S TIP

The weight of rice increases about two
and a half times after cooking.

1 Pat dry the prawns with kitchen
paper. Beat the eggs with a pinch of the
salt and a few pieces of spring onion.

2 Heat half the oil in a wok, add the
pork and stir-fry until golden. Add the
prawns and cook for 1 minute, then add
the soy sauce and rice wine or sherry.
Remove from the heat and keep warm.

3 Heat the remaining oil in the wok and
lightly scramble the eggs. Add the rice
and stir with chopsticks to make sure
that each grain of rice is separated.

4 Add the remaining salt and spring
onions, the stir-fried prawns, pork and
peas. Toss well over the heat to
combine and serve either hot or cold.

QUICHE LORRAINE

THIS CLASSIC QUICHE FROM EASTERN FRANCE HAS SOME DELIGHTFUL, TRADITIONAL CHARACTERISTICS THAT ARE OFTEN FORGOTTEN IN MODERN RECIPES, NAMELY VERY THIN PASTRY, A REALLY CREAMY AND LIGHT, EGG-RICH FILLING, AND SMOKED BACON.

SERVES FOUR TO SIX

INGREDIENTS

175g/6oz/1½ cups plain (all-purpose) flour, sifted
115g/4oz/½ cup unsalted butter, at room temperature, diced
3 eggs, plus 3 yolks
6 smoked streaky (fatty) bacon rashers (strips), rinds removed
300ml/½ pint/1¼ cups double (heavy) cream
25g/1oz/2 tbsp unsalted butter
salt and ground black pepper

1 Place the flour, a pinch of salt, butter and 1 egg yolk in a food processor and process until blended. Tip out on to a floured surface and bring together into a ball. Leave to rest for 20 minutes.

2 Lightly flour a deep 20cm/8in round flan tin (quiche pan), and place it on a baking sheet. Roll out the pastry and use to line the tin, trimming off any excess. Gently press the pastry into the corners of the tin. If the pastry breaks up, don't worry, just gently push it into shape. Chill for 20 minutes. Preheat the oven to 200°C/400°F/Gas 6.

3 Meanwhile, cut the bacon into thin strips and grill (broil) until the fat runs. Arrange the bacon in the pastry case (shell). Beat together the cream, the remaining eggs, yolks and seasoning, and pour into the pastry case.

4 Bake for 15 minutes, then reduce the heat to 180°C/350°F/Gas 4. Bake for a further 15–20 minutes. When the filling is puffed up and golden brown and the pastry edge crisp, remove from the oven and top with knobs (pats) of butter. Stand for 5 minutes before serving.

COOK'S TIP
To prepare the quiche in advance, bake for 5–10 minutes less than recommended, until the filling is just set. Reheat later at 190°C/375°F/Gas 5 for about 10 minutes.

SPICY SAUSAGE AND CHEESE TORTILLA

A COLOURFUL, SPANISH-STYLE OMELETTE, WHICH IS DELICIOUS HOT OR COLD. CUT INTO WEDGES AND SERVE WITH A FRESH TOMATO AND BASIL SALAD.

SERVES FOUR TO SIX

INGREDIENTS
   75ml/5 tbsp olive oil
   175g/6oz chorizo or spicy sausages,
      thinly sliced
   675g/1½lb potatoes, peeled and
      thinly sliced
   275g/10oz onions, halved and
      thinly sliced
   4 eggs, beaten
   30ml/2 tbsp chopped fresh parsley,
      plus extra to garnish
   115g/4oz/1 cup Cheddar cheese, grated
   salt and ground black pepper

1 Heat 15ml/1 tbsp of the oil in a non-stick frying pan, about 20cm/8in in diameter, and fry the sausage until golden brown and cooked through. Lift out with a slotted spoon and drain on kitchen paper.

2 Add a further 30ml/2 tbsp oil to the pan and fry the potatoes and onions for 2–3 minutes, turning frequently (the pan will be very full). Cover tightly and cook over a gentle heat for about 30 minutes, turning occasionally, until softened and slightly golden.

3 In a mixing bowl, mix the beaten eggs with the parsley, cheese, sausage and plenty of seasoning. Gently stir in the potatoes and onions until well coated, taking care not to break up the potato slices too much.

4 Wipe out the pan with kitchen paper and heat the remaining 30ml/2 tbsp oil. Add the potato mixture and cook over a very low heat, until the egg begins to set. Use a spatula to prevent the tortilla from sticking to the sides.

5 Preheat the grill (broiler) to hot. When the base of the tortilla has set, which should take about 5 minutes, protect the pan handle with foil and place under the grill until the tortilla is set and golden. Cut into wedges and serve garnished with parsley.

CLASSIC CHEESE SOUFFLÉ

A LIGHT, DELICATE, MELT-IN-THE-MOUTH CHEESE SOUFFLÉ MAKES ONE OF THE MOST DELIGHTFUL LUNCH DISHES IMAGINABLE. ALL YOU NEED TO GO WITH IT IS SALAD, A GLASS OF GOOD WINE AND PLENTY OF TIME TO RELAX AND ENJOY A LAZY WEEKEND.

SERVES TWO TO THREE

INGREDIENTS

50g/2oz/¼ cup butter
30–45ml/2–3 tbsp breadcrumbs
200ml/7fl oz/scant 1 cup milk
30g/1¼oz/3 tbsp plain
 (all-purpose) flour
pinch of cayenne pepper
2.5ml/½ tsp mustard powder
50g/2oz mature (sharp) Cheddar
 cheese, grated
25g/1oz/⅓ cup freshly grated
 Parmesan cheese
4 eggs, separated, plus 1 egg white
salt and ground black pepper

2 Heat the milk in a large pan. Add the remaining butter, flour and cayenne, with the mustard powder. Bring to the boil over a low heat, whisking steadily until the mixture thickens to a smooth sauce.

5 Add a few spoonfuls of the beaten egg whites to the sauce to lighten it. Beat well, then tip the rest of the whites into the pan and, with a large metal spoon, gently fold in the egg whites, using a figure-of-eight movement to combine the mixtures.

1 Preheat the oven to 190°C/375°F/ Gas 5. Melt 15ml/1 tbsp of the butter and use to thoroughly grease a 1.2 litre/ 2 pint/5 cup soufflé dish. Coat the inside of the dish with breadcrumbs.

3 Simmer the sauce for a minute or two, then turn off the heat and whisk in all the Cheddar and half the Parmesan. Cool a little, then beat in the egg yolks. Check the seasoning; the mixture should be well seasoned. Set aside.

6 Pour the mixture into the prepared soufflé dish, level the top and, to help the soufflé rise evenly, run your finger around the inside rim of the dish.

7 Place the dish on a baking sheet. Sprinkle the remaining Parmesan over the top of the soufflé mixture and bake for about 25 minutes until risen and golden brown. Serve immediately.

VARIATIONS
• Crumbled blue cheese, such as Stilton, Shropshire Blue or Fourme d'Ambert, will produce a soufflé with a much stronger, sharper flavour.
• This soufflé can also be served as a main meal by adding a few extra ingredients. Try putting a layer of chopped vegetables, such as ratatouille or sautéed mushrooms, at the bottom of the dish before adding the cheese mixture. Bake as in the main recipe.

4 Whisk the egg whites in a large grease-free bowl until they form soft, glossy peaks. Do not overbeat or the whites will become grainy and difficult to fold in.

COOK'S TIP
It is important to serve soufflés the moment they are cooked and taken from the oven. Otherwise, the wonderful puffed top may sink before it reaches the waiting diners.

MAIN MEALS

When you think of main meals, the first ingredient you think of isn't always eggs. However, there are many delicious main dishes whose key ingredient is eggs. The wonderful array of dishes in this chapter takes advantage of the versatile qualities of eggs, either in their whole form or by combining them with other ingredients.

Dishes such as Spaghetti with Eggs, Bacon and Cream, rely on eggs for their rich and creamy sauces, while Smoked Fish Soufflé Pudding uses whisked egg whites to attain its light texture. For a special occasion, Mushroom and Quail's Eggs Gougère or Smoked Salmon and Herb Roulade will make the perfect choice, while Tomato Bread and Butter Pudding is a great winter warmer for a family supper.

SPAGHETTI WITH EGGS, BACON AND CREAM

THIS ITALIAN CLASSIC, FLAVOURED WITH PANCETTA AND A GARLIC AND EGG SAUCE THAT COOKS AROUND THE HOT SPAGHETTI, IS POPULAR WORLDWIDE. IT MAKES A GREAT LAST-MINUTE SUPPER.

3 Meanwhile, cook the spaghetti in a large pan of salted boiling water according to the instructions on the packet until *al dente*.

4 Put the eggs, crème fraîche and grated Parmesan in a bowl. Stir in plenty of black pepper, then beat together well.

5 Drain the pasta thoroughly, tip it into the pan with the pancetta or bacon and toss well to mix.

6 Turn off the heat under the pan, then immediately add the egg mixture and toss thoroughly so that it cooks lightly and coats the pasta.

7 Season to taste, then divide the spaghetti among 4 warmed bowls and sprinkle with ground black pepper. Serve immediately, with extra grated Parmesan handed separately.

COOK'S TIP
You can replace the crème fraîche with either double (heavy) cream or sour cream, if you prefer.

SERVES FOUR

INGREDIENTS
30ml/2 tbsp olive oil
1 small onion, finely chopped
1 large garlic clove, crushed
8 pancetta or rindless smoked
  streaky (fatty) bacon rashers
  (strips), cut into 1cm/½in strips
350g/12oz fresh or dried spaghetti
4 eggs
90–120ml/6–8 tbsp/½ cup
  crème fraîche
60ml/4 tbsp freshly grated
  Parmesan cheese, plus extra
  to serve
salt and ground black pepper

1 Heat the oil in a large pan, add the onion and garlic and fry gently for about 5 minutes until softened.

2 Add the pancetta or bacon to the pan and cook for 10 minutes, stirring.

BAKED PEPPERS WITH EGG AND LENTILS

THESE OVEN-BAKED EGGS WITH A DIFFERENCE MAKE A TASTY SIDE DISH. THEY ARE DELICIOUS SERVED WITH GRILLED FISH OR PORK CHOPS, BUT ALSO MAKE AN EXCELLENT LIGHT MEAL FOR VEGETARIANS.

SERVES FOUR

INGREDIENTS

- 75g/3oz/½ cup Puy lentils
- 2.5ml/½ tsp ground turmeric
- 2.5ml/½ tsp ground coriander
- 2.5ml/½ tsp paprika
- 450ml/¾ pint/1¾ cups chicken or vegetable stock
- 2 large (bell) peppers, halved lengthways and seeded
- a little oil
- 15ml/1 tbsp chopped fresh mint
- 4 eggs
- salt and ground black pepper
- sprigs of coriander (cilantro), to garnish

COOK'S TIP

Use beefsteak tomatoes instead of peppers. Cut the top off and scoop out their middles. Fill and bake as before.

1 Put the lentils in a pan with the spices and stock. Bring to the boil, stirring occasionally, and simmer for 30–40 minutes. If necessary, add more water during cooking.

2 Brush the peppers lightly with oil and place close together on a baking tray. Stir the mint into the lentils, then fill the peppers with the mixture. Preheat the oven to 190°C/375°F/Gas 5.

3 Crack the eggs, one at a time, into a small jug (pitcher) and pour into the middle of a pepper. Stir into the lentils and sprinkle with seasoning. Bake for 10 minutes until the egg white is just set. Garnish with coriander and serve.

VARIATION

Add a little extra flavour to the lentil mixture by adding chopped onion and tomatoes sautéed in olive oil.

COUSCOUS WITH EGGS AND TOMATO SAUCE

MIDDLE EASTERN VEGETARIAN FOOD IS BOTH VARIED AND QUICK, ESPECIALLY WITH THE EASY-TO-USE, READY-PREPARED COUSCOUS THAT IS AVAILABLE NOWADAYS.

SERVES FOUR

INGREDIENTS

675g/1½lb plum tomatoes, chopped
4 garlic cloves, chopped
120ml/4fl oz/½ cup olive oil
½ red chilli, seeded and chopped
10ml/2 tsp soft light brown sugar
4 eggs
1 large onion, chopped
2 celery sticks, finely sliced
50g/2oz/scant ½ cup sultanas
    (golden raisins)
200g/7oz/generous 1 cup ready-to-
    use couscous
350ml/12fl oz/1½ cups hot vegetable
    or chicken stock
salt and ground black pepper

1 Preheat the oven to 200°C/400°F/ Gas 6. Put the tomatoes and garlic in a roasting pan, drizzle with 30ml/2 tbsp of the oil, sprinkle with chopped chilli, sugar and salt and pepper, and roast for 20 minutes until soft.

2 Boil the eggs for 4 minutes, then plunge them straight into cold water and leave in cold running water until cold. Carefully peel off the shells.

3 Put 15–30ml/1–2 tbsp of the olive oil in a large pan and fry the onion and celery until softened. Add the sultanas, couscous and hot stock and set aside until all the liquid has been absorbed. Stir gently, add extra hot stock if necessary and season to taste. Tip the couscous into a large heated serving dish, bury the eggs in the couscous and cover with foil. Keep warm in the oven.

COOK'S TIP
You can use any kind of eggs in this dish: smaller ones such as pheasant, guinea fowl and bantam make an interesting variation. However, they are more difficult to peel. Add 1–2 extra eggs per serving depending on their size.

4 Remove the tomatoes from the oven and push through a sieve. Add 15ml/ 1 tbsp boiling water and 15ml/1 tbsp olive oil to the puréed tomatoes and blend to give a smooth, rich sauce. Spoon a little sauce over the top of each egg. Serve at once, with the remaining sauce handed separately.

TUNA AND EGG GALETTE

THIS FLAKY PASTRY TART COMBINES SOFT-CENTRED EGGS AND A SLIGHTLY PIQUANT FISH FILLING. IT MAKES A WONDERFUL DISH FOR A SUMMER SUPPER AND IS ALSO A GREAT BUFFET-TABLE STANDBY.

SERVES FOUR

INGREDIENTS
2 sheets of ready-rolled puff pastry
flour, for rolling
beaten egg, to glaze
60ml/4 tbsp olive oil
175g/6oz tuna steak
2 onions, sliced
1 red (bell) pepper, seeded
  and chopped
2 garlic cloves, crushed
45ml/3 tbsp capers, drained
5ml/1 tsp grated lemon rind
30ml/2 tbsp lemon juice
5 eggs
salt and ground black pepper
30ml/2 tbsp chopped flat leaf
  parsley, to garnish

1 Preheat the oven to 190°C/375°F/ Gas 5. Lay one sheet of pastry on a floured baking sheet and cut to a 28 × 18cm/11 × /in. Brush with beaten egg.

2 Cut the second sheet of pastry to the same size. Cut out a rectangle from the centre and discard, leaving a 2.5cm/1in border. Carefully lift the border on to the first sheet. Brush the border with beaten egg and prick the base.

3 Bake the pastry case for about 15 minutes until golden and well risen.

COOK'S TIP
If you are using fresh, unfrozen pastry, the remaining rectangle of pastry can be wrapped in clear film and frozen. Allow to defrost at room temperature for one hour before using.

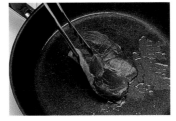

4 Heat 30ml/2 tbsp of the oil in a frying pan and fry the tuna steak for 2–3 minutes on each side until golden but still pale pink in the middle. Transfer to a plate and flake into small pieces.

5 Add the remaining oil to the pan and fry the onions, red pepper and garlic for 6–8 minutes until softened, stirring occasionally. Remove the pan from the heat and stir in the tuna, capers and lemon rind and juice. Season well.

6 Spoon the filling into the pastry case (shell) and level the surface with the back of a spoon. Break the eggs into the filling and return the galette to the oven for about 10 minutes, or until the eggs have just cooked through. Garnish with parsley and serve at once.

COOK'S TIP
To make sure the eggs do not become hard on top during baking, cover the tart with lightly oiled foil.

MUSHROOM <u>AND</u> QUAIL'S EGGS GOUGÈRE

GOUGÈRE IS A POPULAR PASTRY FROM THE BURGUNDY REGION OF FRANCE, WHERE LITTLE BUNS MADE FROM THE SAME PASTRY ARE TOPPED WITH GRUYÈRE CHEESE AND SERVED WITH A GLASS OF WINE. HERE THE GOUGÈRE IS FILLED WITH WILD MUSHROOMS AND TINY, LIGHTLY BOILED QUAIL'S EGGS.

SERVES FOUR TO SIX

INGREDIENTS
    75g/3oz/6 tbsp butter, cut into
      small pieces
    2.5ml/½ tsp salt
    175ml/6fl oz/¾ cup water
    100g/3¾oz/scant 1 cup plain
      (all-purpose) flour, sifted
    4 eggs
    115g/4oz/1 cup Gruyère cheese, grated
    25g/1oz/2 tbsp butter
    1 onion, chopped
    2 celery sticks, sliced
    350g/12oz/4 cups mixed wild
      mushrooms, halved or quartered
    25g/1oz/¼ cup cornflour (cornstarch)
    150ml/¼ pint/⅔ cup red wine and
      water, mixed
    150ml/¼ pint/⅔ cup stock
    dash of Worcestershire sauce
    15ml/1 tbsp chopped flat leaf parsley
    12 quail's eggs

1 Preheat the oven to 220°F/425°F/ Gas 7. In a pan, melt the butter with the salt and water, and bring to the boil. Remove from the heat, add the flour all at once and beat hard with a wooden spoon until it forms a ball.

2 Return the pan to the heat and cook, beating hard, for 1–2 minutes. Leave to cool slightly. Add two of the eggs, beating until the mixture becomes smooth and glossy. Beat in the third egg until smooth, then beat in as much of the fourth egg as you need to attain a smooth, glossy, soft, dropping (pourable) consistency. Beat in half of the Gruyère cheese.

3 Place a round of non-stick baking paper on a baking sheet and place large spoonfuls of the mixture evenly in a circle about 20cm/8in. Place them close together so that they will join up while they cook. Bake for about 35 minutes until well risen and golden all over. Remove from the oven and set aside to cool slightly.

4 Meanwhile, heat the butter in a pan, and fry the onion and celery until softened. Add the mushrooms and cook gently until their juices run. Blend together the cornflour and wine. Add the stock to the mushrooms and gradually stir in the cornflour mixture. Cook gently until thickened. Add the sauce and parsley and cook gently for a few minutes until quite thick.

5 Place the quail's eggs in a pan of cold water, bring to the boil and cook for 1 minute. Cool thoroughly, then peel.

6 To serve, slice the gougère in half horizontally. Fill with the mushrooms and top with the eggs. Replace the top, sprinkle over the remaining cheese and return to the oven until the cheese melts.

SMOKED SALMON AND HERB ROULADE

A LITTLE SMOKED SALMON GOES A LONG WAY IN THE FILLING FOR THIS DELICATELY FLAVOURED ROULADE. MAKE THE ROULADE IN ADVANCE TO GIVE IT TIME TO COOL, BUT DON'T PUT IT IN THE REFRIGERATOR OR IT WILL LOSE ITS LIGHT TEXTURE.

2 Prepare a 33 × 28cm/13 × 11in Swiss (jelly) roll tin (pan). Preheat the oven to 180°C/350°F/Gas 4. Whisk the egg whites, fold into the sauce and pour into the tin. Bake for 12–15 minutes. Leave, covered with greaseproof (waxed) paper, for 10–15 minutes, then tip out on to greaseproof paper sprinkled with grated Parmesan cheese. Allow to cool.

3 Mix together the crème fraîche, chopped smoked salmon, chopped dill and seasoning.

4 Spread over the roulade and roll up, then leave to firm up in a cold place. Sprinkle with the rest of the Parmesan and garnish with lamb's lettuce.

SERVES SIX TO EIGHT

INGREDIENTS
  25g/1oz/2 tbsp butter
  25g/1oz/¼ cup plain
    (all-purpose) flour
  175ml/6fl oz/¾ cup milk, warm
  3 large eggs, separated
  50g/2oz/⅔ cup freshly grated
    Parmesan cheese
  30ml/2 tbsp chopped fresh dill
  30ml/2 tbsp chopped fresh parsley
  150ml/¼ pint/⅔ cup full-fat
    crème fraîche
  115g/4oz smoked salmon, chopped
  salt and ground black pepper
  lamb's lettuce, to garnish

1 Melt the butter in a heavy pan, blend in the flour and cook over a low heat to a thick paste. Then gradually stir in the milk, whisking as it thickens, and cook for 1–2 minutes to make a thick sauce. Stir in the egg yolks, two-thirds of the Parmesan cheese, the herbs and salt and ground black pepper to taste.

COOK'S TIP
Roulades are ideal for entertaining because they can be made in advance. To ring the changes, use other strong-flavoured cheeses, or add cooked fresh salmon, tuna or prawns to the filling instead of Parmesan and smoked salmon.

Spiced Lamb with Soufflé Topping

You will find versions of this dish around the world under different names. In South Africa it is called Bobotee, in India and the East it is Keema per Enda.

SERVES FOUR

INGREDIENTS
  30ml/2 tbsp vegetable oil
    or ghee
  2 onions, finely chopped
  2 large garlic cloves, crushed
  1cm/½in piece fresh root ginger,
    peeled and grated
  15ml/1 tbsp chilli powder
  10ml/2 tsp ground coriander
  5ml/1 tsp ground cumin
  15ml/1 tbsp ground turmeric
  675g/1½lb minced (ground) lamb
  2 large tomatoes, chopped
  4 eggs
  10ml/2 tsp cornflour (cornstarch)
  30–45ml/2–3 tbsp chopped fresh
    coriander (cilantro) or parsley
  salt and ground black pepper
  rice, noodles or baked potatoes
    and a mixed salad, to serve

1 Heat the oil or ghee in a pan and sauté the onion and garlic until soft. Add the ginger and spices and fry for 2 minutes. Add the mince and stir over a high heat until browned.

2 Add 150ml/¼ pint/⅔ cup water and the tomatoes and simmer for about 12 minutes or until the liquid has reduced. Transfer to an ovenproof dish. Preheat the oven to 190°C/375°F/Gas 5.

3 Separate the egg yolks and whites and place in separate bowls. Whisk the yolks with the cornflour and seasoning. Stiffly whisk the egg whites, then fold in the yolks and half the coriander or parsley. Spoon the egg mixture over the mince and cook for 20 minutes or until well risen and golden. Sprinkle with the rest of the coriander or parsley. Serve piping hot with a mixed salad and rice, noodles or baked potatoes.

Tomato Bread and Butter Pudding

This is a great family dish and is ideal when you don't have time to cook on the day because it can be prepared in advance. It makes a wonderful warming supper.

SERVES FOUR

INGREDIENTS
  50g/2oz/4 tbsp butter, softened
  15ml/1 tbsp red pesto sauce
  1 garlic and herb foccacia
  2 large ripe tomatoes, sliced
  150g/5oz mozzarella cheese,
    thinly sliced
  300ml/½ pint/1¼ cups milk
  3 large (US X large) eggs
  5ml/1 tsp fresh chopped oregano,
    plus extra to garnish
  50g/2oz Pecorino Romano or Fontina
    cheese, grated
  salt and ground black pepper

COOK'S TIP
If you like, you could use other cheeses such as Beaufort, Bel Paese or Taleggio, in this pudding.

1 Preheat the oven to 180°C/350°F/ Gas 4. Blend together the butter and pesto sauce in a small bowl. Slice the herb bread and spread one side of each slice with the pesto mixture.

2 In an oval ovenproof dish, layer the bread slices with the mozzarella and tomatoes, overlapping each new layer with the next.

3 Beat together the milk, eggs and oregano, season well and pour over the bread. Leave to stand for 5 minutes.

4 Sprinkle over the grated cheese and bake the pudding in the oven for about 40 minutes or until golden brown and just set. Serve immediately, straight from the dish, sprinkled with more coarsely chopped oregano.

SMOKED FISH SOUFFLÉ PUDDING

THIS SUPERB DISH IS AN INTERESTING CROSS BETWEEN A SOUFFLÉ AND A FISH PIE, SUBSTANTIAL ENOUGH FOR A SUNDAY LUNCH OR A WINTER SUPPER. IT'S EASY TO EAT, SO CHILDREN WILL LOVE IT.

SERVES FOUR TO FIVE

INGREDIENTS
  450g/1lb smoked haddock or cod,
    soaked for 20 minutes in cold water
  350g/12oz cooked, peeled potatoes,
    kept warm
  50g/2oz/4 tbsp butter
  45ml/3 tbsp chopped fresh chives,
    plus extra to garnish
  3 eggs, separated
  15ml/1 tbsp lemon juice
  salt and ground black pepper

COOK'S TIP
For extra flavour, add a splash of dry white vermouth or white wine to the fish poaching water.

1 Preheat the oven to 180°C/350°F/ Gas 4. Drain the smoked haddock or cod, place in a large pan, cover in cold water and bring to simmering point. Poach the fish for 5–7 minutes until it flakes easily. Cool slightly, then drain well and remove the skin and bones.

2 Mash the potatoes thoroughly with the butter, chives, egg yolks and seasoning. Stir in the flaked fish and lemon juice. Whisk the egg whites until stiff and fold in. Spoon into a buttered, deep ovenproof dish and bake for 35 minutes or until well risen and golden on top.

EGG AND GREEN VEGETABLE RISOTTO

THE ADDITION OF EGGS TURNS THIS ITALIAN FAVOURITE INTO A DELICATE, CREAMY DISH. SERVE IT WITH CHUNKS OF COUNTRY BREAD OR A CRISP FENNEL AND RADICCHIO SALAD.

SERVES FOUR

INGREDIENTS
  50g/2oz/¼ cup butter
  1 onion, chopped
  2 garlic cloves, crushed
  225g/8oz/scant 1¼ cups Arborio
    or risotto rice
  600–750ml/1–1¼ pints/2½–3 cups
    good chicken or vegetable
    stock, hot
  3 eggs
  75g/3oz/1 cup freshly grated
    Parmesan cheese
  15ml/1 tbsp lemon juice
  115g/4oz spinach, green cabbage
    or chard, shredded
  salt and ground black pepper

VARIATION
For a country-style risotto, use sorrel instead of spinach. Omit the lemon juice because this vegetable already has a slightly sharp flavour.

1 Melt the butter in a heavy pan. Add the onion and garlic and cook gently until softened, stirring occasionally. Add the rice and stir until thoroughly coated in butter, then pour on 300ml/½ pint/ 1¼ cups of the stock.

COOK'S TIP
If you have leftover rice you can use it in this dish. Omit step 2, then add the eggs, cheese and lemon juice as above and cook gently until soft and creamy. Other green vegetables can be used instead. Try cooked leeks or asparagus.

2 Over a gentle heat, slowly bring the mixture to the boil, then simmer, stirring only once, until the liquid is absorbed. Add another 300ml/½ pint/1¼ cups of stock and cook until all this liquid has been absorbed.

3 Beat together the eggs, cheese, lemon juice, green vegetable and seasoning. Stir into the rice and cook very gently for about 5 minutes, adding more stock if the mixture seems too stiff. The perfect risotto has a soft and creamy texture.

DESSERTS
AND CAKES

So many of our classic desserts and cakes rely on eggs for their rich, creamy
or light textures. Whisked egg whites create the crisp, yet chewy, texture of
Summer Fruit Pavlova, while whole eggs make a delicious creamy filling for
Classic Lemon Tart. Combining whisked egg whites with puréed fruit will
produce delicious Hot Blackberry and Apple Soufflés, while whisked egg
yolks are the key ingredient for Summer Berries in Warm Sabayon Glaze.
Eggs are also essential for a whole range of cakes, from light and
airy Angel Food Cake to tangy Madeira Cake
with Lemon Syrup.

SUMMER FRUIT PAVLOVA

PAVLOVA IS A STUNNING DESSERT AND SIMPLE TO MAKE, TOO. TOP IT WITH RED AND BLACK SOFT SUMMER BERRIES AND PLENTY OF CRÈME FRAÎCHE OR CREAM.

SERVES FOUR

INGREDIENTS
  4 egg whites
  a pinch of salt
  225g/8oz/generous 1 cup caster
    (superfine) sugar
  5ml/1 tsp cornflour (cornstarch)
  15ml/1 tbsp rose water
  300ml/½ pint/1¼ cups crème
    fraîche, or double cream, whipped
  450g/1lb/4 cups mixed soft fruits,
    such as blackcurrants or raspberries
  10ml/2 tsp icing (confectioners')
    sugar, sifted

1 Preheat the oven to 140°C/275°F/ Gas 1. Cut out a 25cm/10in round of greaseproof (waxed) paper and place on a baking sheet.

2 Whisk the egg whites with a pinch of salt in a spotlessly clean bowl until white and stiff, but not crumbly. Slowly add almost all of the sugar, whisking all the time until the mixture forms stiff, glossy peaks.

3 Sift the cornflour over the meringue mixture, then add the rest of the sugar and whisk briefly to combine.

4 Spoon the meringue on to the greaseproof paper round, making a slight indentation in the centre and soft crests around the outside.

5 Bake for 1–1½ hours until the meringue is firm, checking frequently after 1 hour to prevent the meringue overcooking and turning brown.

6 Allow the meringue to cool, then carefully peel off the greaseproof paper from the base. Transfer the meringue to a serving plate.

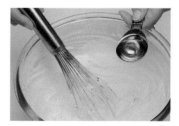

7 To make the filling, mix the crème fraîche or whipped cream with the rose water and spoon into the centre of the meringue. Pile the soft fruits on top and dust with icing sugar. Serve at once.

COOK'S TIPS
• The pavlova meringue can be made in advance and stored in an airtight container or, better still, it can be kept in the freezer.
• Next time you make mayonnaise or a recipe that only requires egg yolks, freeze the unused egg whites, ready for this special dessert.

CLASSIC LEMON TART

THIS IS ONE DISH WHERE THE COLOUR OF THE YOLKS MAKES A REAL DIFFERENCE TO THE COLOUR OF THE TART; THE YELLOWER THE BETTER. THIS TART CAN BE SERVED WARM OR CHILLED AND DECORATED WITH EXTRA LEMON RIND. IT IS VERY LEMONY, SO SERVE WITH CREAM OR VANILLA ICE CREAM.

SERVES EIGHT

INGREDIENTS

150g/5oz/1¼ cups plain (all-purpose) flour, sifted
50g/2oz/½ cup hazelnuts, toasted and finely ground
175g/6oz/scant 1 cup caster (superfine) sugar
115g/4oz/½ cup unsalted butter, softened
4 free-range eggs
finely grated rind of 2 lemons and at least 175ml/6fl oz/¾ cup lemon juice
150ml/¼ pint/⅔ cup double (heavy) cream

COOK'S TIP
Roll the pastry over the loose base of the flan tin, then ease it into the surround.

1 Mix together the flour, nuts and 25g/1oz/2 tbsp sugar, then gently work in the butter and, if necessary, 15–30ml/1–2 tbsp cold water to make a soft dough. Chill for 10 minutes. Roll out the dough and use to line a 20.5cm/8in loose-based flan tin (tart pan). If the pastry is difficult to roll out, push it into the flan tin. Chill for 20 minutes. Preheat the oven to 200°C/400°F/Gas 6.

2 Line the pastry case (shell) with greaseproof (waxed) paper, then fill with baking beans and bake for 15 minutes. Remove the paper and beans, and cook for a further 5–10 minutes until crisp.

3 Beat the eggs, lemon rind and juice, the remaining sugar and cream until well blended. Pour into the pastry case. Bake for about 30 minutes, until just set.

BAKED CARAMEL CUSTARD

MANY COUNTRIES HAVE THEIR OWN VERSION OF THIS CLASSIC DESSERT. KNOWN AS CRÈME CARAMEL IN FRANCE AND FLAN IN SPAIN, THIS CHILLED BAKED CUSTARD HAS A RICH CARAMEL FLAVOUR AND IS WONDERFUL WHEN FRESHLY MADE. SERVE IT WITH EXTRA THICK CREAM AND STRAWBERRIES.

SERVES SIX TO EIGHT

INGREDIENTS
  250g/9oz/1¼ cups granulated sugar
  1 vanilla pod
  425ml/15fl oz/1¾ cups double
    (heavy) cream
  5 large (US X large) eggs, plus
    2 extra yolks
  cream and strawberries, to serve

1 Put 175g/6oz/generous ¾ cup of the sugar in a small heavy pan with just enough water to moisten the sugar. Bring to the boil over a high heat, swirling the pan until the sugar is dissolved completely. Boil for about 5 minutes, without stirring, until the syrup turns a dark caramel colour.

3 Preheat the oven to 160°C/325°F/ Gas 3. With a small sharp knife, carefully split the vanilla pod lengthways and scrape the black seeds into a pan. Add the cream and bring just to the boil over a medium-high heat, stirring frequently. Remove the pan from the heat, cover and set aside for about 20 minutes to cool.

6 Place the dish in a roasting pan and pour in just enough boiling water to come halfway up the side of the dish.

7 Bake the custard for 40–45 minutes until just set. To test whether the custard is set, insert a knife about 5cm/2in from the edge; if it comes out clean, the custard should be ready.

8 Remove the soufflé dish from the roasting pan and leave to cool for at least 30 minutes, then place in the refrigerator and chill overnight.

2 Working quickly, pour the caramel into a 1 litre/1¾ pint/4 cup soufflé dish. Holding the dish with oven gloves, carefully swirl to coat the base and sides with the hot caramel mixture and set aside to cool.

4 In a bowl, whisk the eggs and egg yolks with the remaining sugar for 2–3 minutes until smooth and creamy.

5 Whisk in the hot cream and carefully strain the mixture into the caramel-lined dish. Cover tightly with foil.

VARIATION
For a special occasion, make individual baked custards in ramekin dishes. Coat 6–8 ramekins with the caramel and divide the custard mixture among them. Bake, in a roasting pan of water, for 25–30 minutes or until set. Slice the strawberries and marinate them in a little sugar and a liqueur or dessert wine, such as Amaretto or Muscat wine.

9 To turn out, carefully run a sharp knife around the edge of the dish to loosen the custard.

10 Cover the dish with a serving plate and, holding them together very tightly, invert the dish and plate, allowing the custard to drop down on to the plate.

11 Gently lift one edge of the dish, allowing the caramel to run down over the sides and on to the plate, then carefully lift off the dish. Serve with cream and strawberries.

COLD LEMON SOUFFLÉ WITH ALMONDS

TERRIFIC TO LOOK AT YET EASY TO MAKE, THIS REFRESHING DESSERT SOUFFLÉ IS LIGHT AND MOUTHWATERING, IDEAL FOR THE END OF ANY MEAL.

SERVES SIX

INGREDIENTS
oil, for greasing
grated rind and juice of
  3 large lemons
5 large (US X large) eggs, separated
115g/4oz/½ cup caster
  (superfine) sugar
25ml/1½ tbsp powdered gelatine
450ml/¾ pint/scant 2 cups
  double (heavy) cream
For the almond topping
75g/3oz/¾ cup flaked
  (sliced) almonds
75g/3oz/¾ cup icing
  (confectioners') sugar

1 Wrap a strip of baking parchment around a 900ml/1½ pint/3¾ cup soufflé dish. It should extend 7.5cm/3in above the rim. Tape the strip in place, then tie it around the top of the dish with string. Using a pastry brush, lightly coat the inside of the paper collar with oil.

2 Put the lemon rind and egg yolks in a bowl. Add 75g/3oz/6 tbsp of the caster sugar and whisk thoroughly until the mixture becomes light and creamy.

VARIATIONS
This soufflé is wonderfully refreshing when served semi-frozen. Place the undecorated, set soufflé in the freezer for about an hour. Just before serving, remove from the freezer and decorate with the caramelized almonds. You can also vary the flavour slightly by using the juice and rind of 5 limes.

3 Place the lemon juice in a small heatproof bowl and sprinkle over the gelatine. Set aside for 5 minutes, then place the bowl in a pan of simmering water. Heat, stirring occasionally, until the gelatine has dissolved. Cool slightly, then stir the gelatine and lemon juice into the egg yolk mixture.

4 In a separate bowl, lightly whip the cream to soft peaks. Fold into the egg yolk mixture and set aside.

5 Whisk the whites to stiff peaks. Gradually whisk in the remaining caster sugar until stiff and glossy. Quickly and lightly fold the whites into the yolk mixture. Pour into the prepared dish, smooth the surface and chill for 4–5 hours.

6 To make the almond topping, brush a baking sheet lightly with oil. Preheat the grill (broiler). Scatter the almonds on the baking sheet and sift the icing sugar over. Grill (broil) until the nuts turn golden and the sugar has caramelized.

7 Allow to cool, then remove the almond mixture from the tray with a metal spatula and break it into pieces.

8 When the soufflé has set, carefully peel off the paper. If the paper does not come away easily, hold the blade of a knife against the set soufflé to help it keep its shape, if necessary. Sprinkle the caramelized almonds on top of the soufflé, to serve.

COOK'S TIP
To dissolve the gelatine more quickly, heat the lemon juice and gelatine in a microwave, on full power, in 30 second bursts, stirring between each burst, until it is fully dissolved.

BITTER CHOCOLATE MOUSSES

These rich and extremely delicious mousses are the quintessential French dessert. They are easy to make and can be prepared ahead of time. Use the darkest chocolate you can find for the most intense bitter chocolate flavour.

SERVES EIGHT

INGREDIENTS
  225g/8oz plain (semisweet)
    chocolate, chopped
  60ml/4 tbsp water
  30ml/2 tbsp orange liqueur or brandy
  30g/1oz/2 tbsp unsalted butter, cut
    into small pieces
  4 eggs, separated
  90ml/6 tbsp whipping cream
  1.5ml/¼ tsp cream of tartar
  45ml/3 tbsp caster (superfine) sugar

COOK'S TIP
This dessert depends on good-quality chocolate, so it is worth searching out the best. Brands to look out for include Valrhona or Lindt Excellence.

1 Place the chocolate and water in a heavy pan. Melt over a low heat, stirring. Remove the pan from the heat and whisk in the orange liqueur or brandy and butter. Beat the egg yolks for about 3 minutes until thick and creamy, then slowly beat into the melted chocolate until well blended. Set aside.

2 Whip the cream until soft peaks form and stir a spoonful into the chocolate mixture to lighten it. Fold in the remaining cream.

3 In a clean, grease-free bowl, use an electric mixer to beat the egg whites slowly until frothy. Add the cream of tartar, increase the speed and continue beating until the egg whites form soft peaks. Gradually sprinkle the sugar over and continue beating until the whites are stiff and glossy.

4 Using a rubber spatula or large metal spoon, stir one-quarter of the whites into the chocolate mixture, then gently fold in the remaining whites, cutting down to the bottom, along the sides and up to the top in a semicircular motion until they are just combined. Don't worry about a few white streaks. Gently spoon into a 2 litre/3¼ pint/8 cup dish or into 8 individual dishes. Chill for at least 2 hours until chilled and set.

5 Spoon a little crème fraîche or sour cream over the mousses and decorate with chocolate curls, if you wish.

COFFEE PROFITEROLES

THESE COFFEE AND CHOUX BUNS ARE FILLED WITH LIGHTLY WHIPPED CREAM AND SMOTHERED WITH A LIQUEUR-LACED WHITE CHOCOLATE SAUCE; IT IS AN IRRESISTIBLE COMBINATION.

SERVES SIX

INGREDIENTS
    65g/2½oz/9 tbsp plain
      (all-purpose) flour
    pinch of salt
    50g/2oz/4 tbsp butter
    150ml/¼ pint/⅔ cup freshly
      brewed coffee
    2 eggs, lightly beaten
    250ml/8fl oz/1 cup double
      (heavy) cream
For the white chocolate sauce
    50g/2oz/¼ cup granulated sugar
    150g/5oz white dessert chocolate,
      broken into pieces
    25g/1oz/2 tbsp unsalted butter
    45ml/3 tbsp double (heavy) cream
    30ml/2 tbsp coffee liqueur,
      such as Tia Maria or Kahlúa

1 Preheat the oven to 220°C/425°F/ Gas 7. Sift the flour and salt on to a piece of greaseproof (waxed) paper.

2 Cut the butter into small pieces and place in a pan with the freshly brewed coffee. Bring to a rolling boil, then remove from the heat and shoot in the sifted flour in one go. Beat hard until the mixture leaves the side of the pan, forming a ball of thick paste. Leave to cool for 5 minutes.

3 Gradually add the eggs, beating well between each addition, until the mixture forms a stiff dropping (pourable) consistency. Spoon the mixture into a piping (icing) bag fitted with a 1cm/½ in plain nozzle.

4 Pipe 24 small buns on to a dampened baking sheet, leaving plenty of room between each. Bake for 20 minutes, until well risen and crisp.

5 Remove the buns from the oven and pierce the side of each one with a sharp knife to let out the steam.

6 To make the sauce, put the sugar and 100ml/3½fl oz/½ cup water in a heavy pan, and heat gently until the sugar has completely dissolved. Bring to the boil and simmer for 3 minutes.

7 Remove the pan from the heat, and add the white chocolate and butter, stirring constantly until smooth. Stir in the double cream and liqueur.

8 To assemble the profiteroles, whip the cream until it forms soft peaks. Spoon into a piping bag and fill the buns through the slits in their sides. Arrange on individual plates and pour over a little of the sauce, either warm or at room temperature. Serve the remaining sauce separately in a jug (pitcher).

SUMMER BERRIES <u>IN</u> WARM SABAYON GLAZE

*THIS LUXURIOUS COMBINATION OF SUMMER BERRIES UNDER A LIGHT AND FLUFFY ALCOHOLIC SAUCE IS
LIGHTLY BROWNED TO FORM A CRISP, CARAMELIZED TOPPING.*

<u>SERVES FOUR</u>

INGREDIENTS
   450g/1lb/4 cups mixed summer
      berries, or soft fruit
   4 egg yolks
   50g/2oz/¼ cup vanilla sugar or
      caster (superfine) sugar
   120ml/4fl oz/½ cup liqueur, such as
      Cointreau, kirsch or Grand Marnier,
      or a white dessert wine
   icing (confectioners') sugar, sifted,
      and mint leaves, to decorate

COOK'S TIP
If you want to omit the alcohol, use a
pure juice substitute such as grape,
mango or apricot.

1 Arrange the fruit in 4 heatproof
dishes. Preheat the grill (broiler).

2 Whisk the yolks in a large bowl with
the sugar and liqueur or wine. Place
over a pan of hot water and whisk
constantly until thick, fluffy and pale.

3 Pour equal quantities of the sauce
into each dish. Place under the grill for
1–2 minutes until just turning brown.
Sprinkle the fruit with icing sugar and
scatter with mint leaves just before
serving, if you like. Add an extra splash
of liqueur, if you like.

HOT BLACKBERRY AND APPLE SOUFFLÉS

THE DELICIOUSLY TART FLAVOURS OF BLACKBERRY AND APPLE COMPLEMENT EACH OTHER PERFECTLY TO MAKE A LIGHT, MOUTHWATERING AND SURPRISINGLY LOW-FAT, HOT DESSERT.

MAKES SIX

INGREDIENTS

  butter, for greasing
  150g/5oz/¾ cup caster (superfine)
    sugar, plus extra for dusting
  350g/12oz/3 cups blackberries
  1 large cooking apple, peeled and
    finely diced
  grated rind and juice of 1 orange
  3 egg whites
  icing (confectioners') sugar,
    for dusting

1 Preheat the oven to 200°C/400°F/ Gas 6. Grease six 150ml/¼ pint/⅔ cup soufflé dishes with butter and dust with caster sugar, shaking out any excess.

2 Put a baking sheet in the oven to heat. Cook the blackberries, diced apple and orange rind and juice in a pan for 10 minutes or until the apple has pulped down well. Press through a sieve into a bowl. Stir in 50g/2oz/¼ cup of the caster sugar. Set aside to cool.

3 Put a spoonful of the fruit purée into each prepared dish and smooth the surface. Set the dishes aside.

4 Whisk the egg whites in a large grease-free bowl until they form stiff peaks. Very gradually whisk in the remaining caster sugar to make a stiff, glossy meringue mixture.

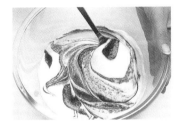

5 Fold in the remaining fruit purée and spoon the flavoured meringue into the prepared dishes. Level the tops with a knife or spatula, and run a table knife around the edge of each dish.

6 Place the dishes on the hot baking sheet and bake for 10–15 minutes until the soufflés have risen well and are lightly browned. Dust the tops with icing sugar and serve immediately.

COOK'S TIP
Running a table knife around the inside edge of the soufflé dishes before baking helps the soufflés to rise evenly without sticking to the rim of the dish.

ANGEL FOOD CAKE

THIS IS AN AMERICAN CLASSIC. IT IS SIMILAR TO A WHISKED SPONGE CAKE; THE TEXTURE IS SPRINGY, BUT SLIGHTLY STICKY, AND THE COLOUR IS SNOWY WHITE. THE CREAM OF TARTAR HELPS TO STIFFEN THE EGG WHITES, AND THE ADDITION OF THE SUGAR FORMS A LIGHT MERINGUE MIXTURE.

SERVES TWENTY

INGREDIENTS
    65g/2½oz/5 tbsp plain (all-purpose)
      flour, sifted
    15ml/1 tbsp cornflour (cornstarch)
    225g/8oz/generous 1 cup sugar
    10 egg whites
    5ml/1 tsp cream of tartar
    5ml/1 tsp vanilla essence (extract)
For the frosting
    115g/4oz/½ cup sugar
    2 egg whites
    10ml/2 tsp golden (light corn) syrup
    2.5ml/½ tsp vanilla essence
    zest of 1 orange, to decorate

2 In a large, grease-free bowl, whisk the egg whites with the cream of tartar until stiff. Gradually whisk in the remaining sugar, 15ml/1 tbsp at a time, until the mixture becomes thick and glossy.

5 Slowly pour the syrup, in a steady stream, into the centre of the egg whites, whisking continuously, until the mixture becomes thick and glossy. Beat in the golden syrup and vanilla essence, and continue beating for 5 minutes until the frosting is cooled.

1 Preheat the oven to 180°C/350°F/ Gas 4. In a large bowl, sift together the flour, cornflour and 50g/2oz/¼ cup of the sugar three times, so the texture is very, very light.

3 Gently fold the sifted flour and the vanilla essence into the whisked egg whites until combined, and transfer to a 25cm/10in non-stick ring mould. Bake for 35–40 minutes until risen and golden. Remove from the oven, invert the cake in its tin on to a wire rack, and leave to cool.

4 To make the frosting, heat the sugar and 60ml/4 tbsp water in a small pan, stirring constantly until the sugar dissolves. Increase the heat and boil until the temperature reaches 115°C/ 240°F on a sugar thermometer. As soon as this temperature is reached, whisk the egg whites until very stiff and dry.

6 Lift the tin off the cooled cake and place the cake on a serving plate or turntable. Spread the frosting over the the cake, using a metal spatula to make a swirling pattern.

7 To decorate the cake, sprinkle over the orange zest.

COOK'S TIP
This success of this very light cake relies on the care taken during its preparation. It is important to sift the dry ingredients three times and to whisk the egg whites to the right consistency. Make sure you do not overbeat the egg whites. They should form soft peaks, not be crumbly, so that the air bubbles can expand further during the cooking time and help the cake to rise.

VARIATION
For a chocolate version of this cake, replace 25g/1oz/2 tbsp of the flour with cocoa powder.

HUNGARIAN FRUIT CAKE

THIS RECIPE PRODUCES A WONDERFULLY LIGHT, WHITE CAKE THAT KEEPS VERY WELL, IF TIGHTLY WRAPPED. IT IS DELICIOUS SERVED SLIGHTLY WARM AS A DESSERT WITH A RICH PLUM OR FRUIT SAUCE OR EVEN A FRESH EGG CUSTARD.

SERVES EIGHT TO TEN

INGREDIENTS
    oil, for greasing
    7 egg whites
    175g/6oz/generous ¾ cup caster
    (superfine) sugar
    115g/4oz/1 cup flaked (sliced)
    almonds, toasted
    115g/4oz/¾ cup sultanas
    (golden raisins)
    grated rind of 1 lemon
    160g/5½oz/1⅓ cups plain
    (all-purpose) flour, sifted,
    plus extra for flouring
    75g/3oz/6 tbsp unsalted
    butter, melted

1 Preheat the oven to 180°C/350°F/ Gas 4 and grease and flour a 1kg/2¼lb loaf tin (pan). Whisk the egg whites until very stiff, but not crumbly. Fold in the sugar gradually, then the almonds, sultanas and lemon rind.

2 Fold the flour and butter into the egg whites. Tip the mixture into the tin, and bake for about 45 minutes until well risen and pale golden brown. Cool for a few minutes in the tin, then turn out and serve warm or cold, in slices.

MADEIRA CAKE <u>WITH</u> LEMON SYRUP

THIS SUGAR-CRUSTED CAKE IS SOAKED IN LEMON SYRUP, SO IT STAYS MOIST AND IS STEEPED WITH TANGY CITRUS FLAVOUR. SERVE IT SLICED WITH TEA.

SERVES TEN

INGREDIENTS

  250g/9oz/1 cup plus 2 tbsp
    butter, softened
  225g/8oz/generous 1 cup
    caster (superfine) sugar
  5 eggs
  275g/10oz/2½ cups plain (all-
    purpose) flour, sifted
  30ml/2 tbsp baking powder
  salt
For the sugar crust
  60ml/4 tbsp lemon juice
  15ml/1 tbsp golden (light corn) syrup
  30ml/2 tbsp granulated sugar

COOK'S TIP

Make double the quantity of cake. Omit the syrup from one and leave plain. Simply cool, wrap and freeze.

1 Preheat the oven to 180°C/350°F/ Gas 4. Grease a 1kg/2¼lb loaf tin (pan). Beat the butter and sugar until light and creamy, then gradually beat in the eggs.

2 Mix the sifted flour, baking powder and salt, and fold in gently. Spoon into the prepared tin, level the top and bake for 1¼ hours, until a skewer pushed into the middle comes out clean.

3 Remove the cake from the oven and, while still warm and in the tin, use a skewer to pierce it several times right the way through. Warm together the lemon juice and syrup, add the sugar and immediately spoon over the cake, so the flavoured syrup soaks through but leaves some sugar crystals on the top. Chill the cake for several hours or overnight before serving.

EGG INFORMATION AND SUPPLIERS

AUSTRALIA

Australian Egg Industry
   Association
PO Box 569
Hurstville
NSW 1481
Tel: 612 9570 9222
Fax: 612 9570 9763

Australian Poultry Industries
   Association
PO BOX 579
North Sydney
NSW 2059
Tel: 02 9929 4077
Fax: 02 9925 0627

Specialist egg producers

Arrawarra Ostrich Farm
Margaret Withnall
Lot 6
Alkoomie Place
Wilton
NSW 2571
Tel: 0246 308244

David Jones
Gourmet Food
65–77 Market Street
Sydney
NSW 2000
Tel: 612 9266 5544

Farm Pride Foods Ltd
551 Chandler Road
Keysborough
VIC 3173
Tel: 613 9798 7077
Fax: 613 9798 3824
www.farmpride.com.au

Five Star Gourmet Foods
13–16 Willoughby Road
Crows Nest
NSW 2065
Tel: 612 9438 5666
Email: fivestargourmet@
   bigpond.com

Pace Farms Pty Ltd
Richmond Road
Dean Park
NSW 2761
Tel: 612 9626 9744
Fax: 612 9626 3923

CANADA

Canadian Egg and Poultry
   Processors Council
1545 Carling Avenue
Suite 400
Ottowa
Ontario K12 8PG
Tel: 613 724 6605
Fax: 613 724 4577

Manitoba Egg Producers
18 Scurfield Blvd
Winnipeg
Manitoba R3Y 1G3
Tel: 204 488 4888
Fax: 204 488 3544

UNITED KINGDOM

British Domesticated Ostrich
   Association
Beech House
Winskill
Penrith
Cumbria CA10 1PD
Tel: 01768 881 881

British Egg Industry
   Council
Suite 101
Albany House
324–326 Regent Street
London W1R 5AA
Tel: 020 7580 7172

British Egg Information
   Service
Cameron Choat & Partners
Bury House
126–128 Cromwell Road
London SW7 4ET
Tel: 020 7370 7411

British Goose Information
   Bureau
Lime Tree Studio
Pulham Market
Diss
Norfolk IP21 4XR
Tel: 01379 608 151

British Goose Producers'
   Association
Imperial House
15–19 Kingsway House
London WC2B 6UA
Tel: 020 7240 9889

British Nutrition Foundation
High Holborn House
52–54 High Holborn
London EC1V 6RQ
Tel: 020 7404 6504

Duck Information Service
Thames View House
6 St Peter's Road
Twickenham
Middlesex TW1 1QX
Tel: 020 8892 2720

Duck Producer's
   Association
High Holborn House
52–54 High Holborn
London WC1V 6SX
Tel: 020 7242 4683
Fax: 020 7831 0624

International Egg Commission
Suite 105
Albany House
324–326 Regent Street
London W1R 5AA

OSGROW 2000 (Ostrich
   Produce)
Tybroughton Hall
Whitchurch
Shropshire SY13 3BB
Tel: 01948 780 654

RSPCA Freedom Food
Farm Animal Welfare
   Labelling Scheme
The Causeway
Horesham
West Sussex RH12 1H6
Tel: 01403 264 181

Supercook Dried Egg Products
Brandway Group
Bishopdyke Road
Sherburn-in-Elmet
Leeds LS25 6JA
Tel: 01977 684 937

Specialist egg producers

Daylay Foods
The Moor
Bilsthorp
Nr Newark
Nottinghamshire NG22 8TS
Tel: 01623 870 384

Free-range and organic suppliers

Bushwacker Wholefoods
132 King Street
London W6
Tel: 020 8748 2061

Chatsworth Farm Shop
Dilsey, Bakewell
Derbyshire DE45 1UF
Tel: 01246 583 392

The Fresh Food Company
326 Portobello Road
London W10 5RU
Tel: 020 8969 0351

The Game Centre
1 Petersfield Rd
Greatham, Nr Liss
Hampshire GU33 6AA
Tel: 01420 538 162

Graig's Farm Organics
Dolau
Llandrindod Wells
Powys LD1 5TL
Tel: 01597 851 655

North Acomb Farm Shop
Stocksfield-on-Tyne
Northumberland
NE43 7UF
Tel: 01661 843 181

Roseden Farm Shop
Wooperton
Alnwick
Northumberland NE66 4XU
Tel: 01668 217 271

UNITED STATES

American Egg Board
1460 Renaissance Drive
Park Ridge
Illinois 60068
Tel: 847 296 7043
Fax: 847 296 7007

The American Ostrich
  Association
PO Box 162627
Fort Worth
Texas 76161
Tel: 817 624 3322
Fax: 817 624 2047

The Virginia Ostrich
  Association
Memorial Building
Suite 122
610 North Main Street
Blacksburg
Virginia 24060–3349
Tel: 540 951 2559

California Egg
  Commission
2131 S. Grove Avenue
Suite D
Ontario
California 91761

Egg Nutrition Centre
1050 17th Street, NW
Suite 500
Washington DC 20036
Tel: 202 833 8850
Fax: 202 463 0102

Georgia Egg Producers
Atlanta State Farmers' Market
16 Forest Parkway
Forest Park
Georgia 30297
Tel: 404 363 7661

US Poultry and Egg
  Association
1530 Cooledge Road
Tucker
Georgia 3084–7303
Tel: 770 493 9401

ACKNOWLEDGEMENTS

The author would like to thank the following for their assistance with the research and historical information: John Farrant at *Poultry World Magazine* and Emma Powell at The Egg Information Service, and also Nicola Fletcher, Christine France, Deh-Ta Hseung, Sue Lawrence, Alan Long, Margaret Shaida and Ruth Watson. The author would also like to thank the following suppliers for their generous loan of props: David Mellor, 4 Sloane Square, London SW1; Divertimenti, 139–141 Fulham Road, London SW3 6SD; Kenwood Ltd, New Lane, Havant, Hampshire PO9 2NH; Kitchen Aid Europa Inc., Brussels, Belgium, c/o Kate Wild, 22 Brackenbury Road, London W6 0BA; Lakeland Ltd, Alexandra Buildings, Windermere, Cumbria LA23 1BQ; Magimix UK Ltd, 115a High Street, Godalming, Surrey GU7 1AQ; Tefal UK Ltd, 11–49 Station Road, Langley, Slough, Berkshire SL8 8DR; and Teflon Classics, Classic Housewares Ltd, Imperial Mill, Liverpool Road, Burnley, Lancashire BB12 6HH.

All recipe pictures are by Amanda Heywood and all reference pictures are by Steve Moss, except for the following: p6b, The Great Egg Question: Sketches at a Poultry Farm, from *The Illustrated London News*, 2nd April 1887 (engraving) by English School (19th century), Private Collection/ Bridgeman Art Library; p6t, Ms 1175 f59r, Women Buying Eggs (vellum), Vieil Rentier d'Audenarde (1291–1302), Bibliotheque Royale de Belgique/Bridgeman Art Library; p18 and p19t, The Egg Information Service.

INDEX

NOTES

NOTES

NOTES

NOTES